As It Is

As It Is

Raymond G Floodgate

authorHOUSE®

AuthorHouse™
1663 Liberty Drive
Bloomington, IN 47403
www.authorhouse.com
Phone: 1-800-839-8640

First published by AuthorHouse   09/23/2011

ISBN: 978-1-4567-9856-7 (sc)
ISBN: 978-1-4567-9857-4 (ebk)

Printed in the United States of America

Contents

* * *

Introduction

For many years I have understood the fundamental reasons of why we are here on this world. Although my understandings were initially instinctive, I worked very hard using meditation and contemplation techniques and asked many questions to take these insights further. I felt that I needed to gain more knowledge and wisdom about this subject.

The answers to these questions did not just come to me in a flash of inspiration. It took me over thirty five years of study in order to gain a better understanding of why we *really* come to the Earth.

Why go to all that trouble you may ask? I know I could have found more exciting things to do with my life—or perhaps you may even say 'get a life'?

It has never ceased to amaze me how few people on this world even bother to think about why we are here or even consider where we have come from or how we arrived on this world.

Human beings are naturally inquisitive and born with an enquiring mind. However, I would suggest that, through my own experience of living with and talking to people, I would say that there are probably less than 5% of the 6.3 billion people on this world who are aware that there are questions to be asked, and even less who know that there are answers to be found. It would seem that the majority of the planet's inhabitants are quite happy to just drift along oblivious of where they have come from, why they are here or even where they are going when it is time to leave this world. I have also discovered that there is a large proportion of the population who think that "*when you're dead, you're dead*".

Throughout this book I shall be taking a look at why this is *not* the case and looking at some of the questions that we need to ask and where the answers are likely to come from.

It has been known by the modern world for thousands of years that ancient civilisations had the knowledge and ability to change the course of their lives at will and that they could also acquire, by the use of life-force energy and affirmations, any possessions they desired. I will be showing you how to get what you want in this life in a later chapter.

I will not apologise for repeating myself in several places in this book as I believe that repetition is the key to learning and the first step to acquiring wisdom.

Astronomy

I would like to start this book from the beginning so what better place is there than looking at the Universe and its contents. This is where it all started for us and everybody who shares this little bit of space.

The subject of Astronomy, Space and the Universe is immense and an on-going one. We think we know a lot about the universe we live in, and it is true we have come along in leaps and bounds in recent years but, in reality, we have barely scratched the surface.

One reason we know so little is due to our size. We are tiny compared to everything around us and it takes us such a long time to get anywhere. The information that we retrieve from the universe comes mainly from analysing photographs from space and theorising. As an example, let us look at our solar system. To visit the other planets of our solar system it would take us many years of space travel to get there and an equally long time to get back.

Just think of this, Proximus Centauri, the nearest star to us other than our own sun, is 4.2 light years away which, when said quickly, doesn't sound very far but to get there it would take 4.2 years if we were able to travel at the speed of light (186,000 miles per second or about *6 trillion miles* per year). Unfortunately we are not even capable of reaching speeds of 50,000 miles per hour (*at the time of writing*) which if we could, would take us 767.1 lifetimes to get there (based on a lifespan of 75 years or to put it another way 19,177.5 generations) and that is without the journey back.

If a colony of people were to travel to Proximus Centauri, it is unlikely that their descendants, on the return journey to earth, would have anything in common with us when arriving home; if indeed they would even think of this as their home. Even their physical appearance may have changed due to the limited space and low gravitational environment they were born to. Their skeletal structure may have developed differently from that of our own to compensate for the low gravity they were living in. Also, travelling for many hundreds of years away from the Earth and having no contact with the native tongue, their language would almost certainly have undergone changes, much the same as we see the English that is spoken today is markedly different from English spoken a mere three or four hundred years ago so communication could therefore be difficult. When you think that this is a short trip in universal terms, and we are only travelling to our nearest neighbouring star system, the distances become mind-boggling when considering travelling even further afield.

Where do we fit in our universe?

Our home resides within the solar system along with our other seven neighbouring planets (Pluto is no longer regarded as a planet and has been down-graded to that of a mere asteroid). So, the Earth and its seven neighbours are in orbit around our sun which sits around 28,000 light years from the galactic centre in the Orion arm area of our galaxy, the Milky Way. The Milky Way is a spiral galaxy containing approximately 200 billion stars, one of which is our sun. As stars go, our sun is just a medium size average star, nothing special in universal terms although to us it is everything.

The closest galaxy to the Milky Way is the Andromeda galaxy which is 2.5 million light years away. It is also a spiral galaxy and is roughly the same size and mass as the Milky Way. These two galaxies are a part of a number of other galaxies that reside in this area of the universe and are called the Local Group. The Local Group of galaxies is in itself a member of a larger group of galaxies called the Virgo Super Cluster. The Virgo Super Cluster covers an area of space which is 110 million light years across its diameter. There are millions of other super clusters in the observable universe. The universe known to us so far is so vast that we are unable to see beyond its boundaries.

So, here we are on our little planet, going around our little sun, totally full of our own importance and arrogance. We carry a large aggressive chip on our shoulders while supporting an over-inflated ego. We are God's 'chosen children', created by God, in the image of God and therefore we must be special. When in actual fact, in the real scheme of things, we are here for less than a nano second in real time and most of everything we know has only meaning for us *here* and will only be relevant in these times.

The vastness of this universe should give us a clue as to how important we really are. We are one of the tinniest parts of this massive universe but with help and guidance which we so badly need right now, we will grow strong intellectually, spiritually and emotionally. We can then begin to look forward to a brighter future, where we will be the ones giving help and guidance to others in their time of need.

Why are we here?

Well, that is a leading question! Every one of us here on this world today is here because they want to be. Some of you may disagree with this statement, especially if you've just crashed the car, had your house repossessed or perhaps your spouse and children have just left you and taken what little money and possessions you had. Maybe you have lost your job or your business has gone bust leaving you in a state of bankruptcy or perhaps you are currently serving a prison sentence.

I could go on writing all day about the grief, heartache, pain, injustice, poverty and downright misery that we all have to suffer while on this world but, nevertheless, it's true. We are all here, each and every one of us not just because we want to be here, but because we need to be here, we need come to a world like this. Why? *To learn* my friend! I will say it again just in case there is any misunderstanding, *we are here to learn.*

Ok, so we are here to learn. This may lead you to wonder what on earth you are supposed to be learning. You probably thought that you were taught everything you needed to know while you were at school and you may now be putting that knowledge and education to good use, but there are still many lessons that can only be learnt through experiencing life's numerous challenges.

You may also be settled in a good career with excellent prospects, have a wonderful marriage and family and feel that life is good. So what else is there left to learn and why? *Well, here beginneth the first lesson.*

Think of this world as a school and one where we are unable to go home at the end of the day. The school gates are closed—only to be opened at the end of this lifespan when, all things being equal, we have gained enough knowledge from this visit to enable us to move on. You may have heard the expression. "When you're dead, you are dead"? Well, not so my friend. When it is time to move on, our body will die but *we* will still be very much alive.

"Do Unto Others"

Religion teaches us about spiritual matters and how to conduct ourselves while in the presence of others *"do unto others as you would have them do unto you"*. Yes, that's very good advice, but it's not that simple. We cannot have the whole of the world's population *"doing unto others"*, it just wouldn't work. Yes it's true, being kind and considerate to all beings would make the world a far better place to live but we are not here to live in ideal conditions, well certainly not on this world anyway. It may be a lovely place, also a pleasant location to visit for a while, but this is not a holiday camp, far from it. It is a place of learning and the only way that we are able to learn at this stage of our evolution it would seem, is through adversity, hard times and getting a good slap occasionally. Fortunately, very few people *"do unto others"*, and rightly so.

We need to understand that on a world like this, learning covers every aspect of life. We need to experience the *whole* story. How would it be possible to know what good is if we were unable to understand what it is to be bad. How indeed could we know what is pleasant if we haven't experienced unpleasant. Just by way of an example, if a car battery had just one connection, let's say a positive terminal, it would be useless and impossible for it to work. It must also have a negative terminal to complete the electrical circuit, so when wires are attached to it, it will then let the electrical current flow. You cannot have one without the other. It is the same with life on this world, we cannot learn only half the lesson we need to know both sides of the story. You must have the complete picture, negative and positive, good and bad, happy and unhappy. There is no other way. We come to this world to learn and for that purpose only. We need to have a balanced education, this means taking the good with the bad, the happy with the sad and the pleasant with the thoroughly disgusting. Besides, it gives us a chance to have a good old moan every now and again, *as long as we don't make a career out of it!*

So what are the lessons? Who are the teachers? And where is the syllabus? These are all valid questions, so let us have a look at them and see what this is all about.

- *The Lessons*

     The lessons we are given to learn while here on Earth are in the form of a 'things to do list' or in this case, a' things to learn list', which is put together by our Higher Self, guides and spiritual helpers in preparation for our visit here. This list contains the items that will help us acquire the knowledge we need from the experiences we will have, as we go through life. Some experiences are pleasant, happy occasions that are a joy to learn from but, generally, this type of lesson can be learned with no real effort on our part, i.e. interacting with friends, family and people we can rely on and trust to help us when we are going through troubled times. Learning from the people we feel comfortable with is still knowledge gained but it comes easily to us.

     Lessons of a different nature are learnt from people we meet but with whom we are not comfortable or compatible with i.e. people whom we may find untrustworthy, aggressive, loud, and boastful or even those who are thoroughly obnoxious. They all have a hand in helping us to progress.

- *The Teachers*

Everyone we interact with during our lifetime be they human, animal or plant life will be our teacher. They will come into our life just when we need them and then leave when their job is done. If we are able to recognise the help that they are offering, it will not only solve our current problems but we will also learn humility and gratitude by accepting their help. They, in turn, will also learn by helping us, for it's a two-way thing, giving and receiving. They give their help unconditionally and get a feeling of well-being and gratitude inside, as their bodily vibrations increase and you will gain a sense of respect towards that person as they may have gone out of their way or even suffered a little hardship just to help you.

In any interaction between life forms on this world whether it be good or bad, both parties will always learn. Both parties will also be the teacher as we all learn from each other.

- *The Syllabus*

There is no syllabus, at least not on this world. We sort out the things we need to learn *before* we come down to this world, then when we arrive here most of the memories from our previous lives and the lessons learned are temporarily erased from our conscious memory and are not accessible to us as they are not required in this life. They are stored in that great computer in your head called the sub-conscious mind in a folder named '*for future reference only'*.

"Well, how does that work?" Just think about it for a moment. It would be pointless coming down here knowing exactly what it is we need to learn. It would be like going into an exam room already knowing what the questions were beforehand. If we knew the questions before taking an exam, we would only need to learn the answers to be able to pass it. We could even pass with distinction but we would know very little about the subject. To know everything about the subject of study, we would have to do just that, study it. Learn everything about it in every minute detail and look at the subject from every angle so that when we go into that exam room we go in with confidence, knowing that we have worked hard and have all the knowledge required to sail through the exam, no matter how difficult the questions.

When we are born to this world or any other world for that matter, we come down with what would seem to be a blank sheet, an empty hard drive so to speak, and there are two reasons why this happens:

1.   We learn from the beginning every time we come here and we start without any clues what-so-ever. We will

then get an all-round more in-depth education. There will always be lots of mistakes made on our way along the path of life and it's through these mistakes that we will experience our greatest successes and which will take us higher up the ladder of evolution, so making us the people we need to be.

2. It would be cruel indeed for anyone to be expected to start a new life on Earth knowing that, in a previous life, they were an influential multi-billionaire with excellent health, intelligence and every imaginable comfort, together with a loving family and good friends, living the perfect stress-free life (that most of us only dream about) whereas in this, their present life, they may be crippled and blind, living in great pain while also dealing with the immense stresses that poverty and loneliness bring. It must be difficult coping with a life like this even without the knowledge of who we were in a previous existence.

Would you want to know who you used to be or know who you are going to be in a future life? Do you think that if you were honest with yourself you would really be happy to stay here struggling, suffering and totally unhappy with your lot, knowing that when your next life comes along you will be rich, famous and a wonderful person? No, I don't think so. It would be really tempting to end it all now and get this life over and done with so that you could get straight on with all the good stuff coming your way.

(Incidentally, suicide is never a good option no matter how bad you think your circumstances are, things will get even worse for you should you wish to try it).

So you see, there will always have to be rules and regulations exactly as it was when you were at school. If they had told you what it was going to be like before you went to school you probably wouldn't have gone, given the choice. It's the same with life on Earth. Let's be fair, it's not exactly a barrel of laughs down here is it? If you knew about the grief you were letting yourself in for before you came down here you probably wouldn't have wanted to come, given the choice.

As I have already mentioned, coming to this world is our choice and ours alone.

Even though we don't know what lessons we are supposed to be learning while we are here, we are never left on our own, ever. Always at every step of our journey through this life there is someone there to guide us. This may not be apparent to us most of the time. In fact, there are times when we will feel so lonely and frightened it is easy to think that we are the loneliest person on this world. This happens to everyone at some point in their lives but even in times of utter loneliness and despair there is always somebody watching over us. These testing periods of our lives are teaching us the lessons we need to learn. As I have already said, the hardest lessons are normally learnt through adversity and they can be the most important things we will learn in this life, helping us to progress quicker and further, so reducing the number of times we need to come to a world like this.

Why is there so much suffering and heartache on this world? Everybody seems to have one problem after another and sometimes we are left wondering if it will ever end. It seems strange that two of the most used phrases, no matter what country we go to, are "No Worries" and "No Problem" when there are obviously more worries and problems around than anything else. We are strange folk indeed.

Coming down here to this world (*if indeed we do actually come down*) doesn't seem to be a particularly attractive opportunity considering we will already know the grief we are letting ourselves in for when we arrive. So, why do we decide to do it? We come down to worlds like the Earth because we are given the all-round opportunities we need to help us progress. We are provided with all the tools necessary to learn from. These tools will also give us a vast range of experiences from which we can gain all the knowledge and wisdom we need to take home with us when the school gates are eventually opened and we leave this world.

You may ask "What's all this about tools?" I'm sure the nurse didn't say to my Mum when I was born "Oh you've had a lovely baby boy and here is his bag of tools"!

Let us look at what we are given when we are born. Firstly we have our body, this is quite an important physical tool to have, (incidentally *we* are not our body but the spark of life inside it). The type of body we get mostly depends on what things we need to learn while we are here. There's no point in being born into an English body when the lifestyle we have come here to learn about is as a Massai tribesman in Africa and equally, there is no point in being born in Africa when you need to live as an Inuit Eskimo in the Canadian Arctic Circle. We will always be given the right tools to work with when we come down to this planet. These tools will give us the best chance of achieving the goals we set ourselves when we arrive here. As well as our body let us see what other tools we may have at our disposal?

Tools

Greed is the perfect tool to have when we've come here to learn how to acquire and hoard money and possessions. When greed is programmed into our brain for this use, it will help us to maintain the right frame of mind we will need to achieve this particular goal. Although greed is normally associated with money, it can also apply to anything we have of value in our possession and are not prepared to share with others.

Anger is a tool that has two main attributes attached to it:

(1)   It teaches the person who has come here to learn about anger, to be forthright in an aggressive way and to show displeasure with something or someone they disagree with. People with anger problems pressurise

and manipulate others by creating fear in them in order to obtain what they want.

(2)   We can also be given this tool so that we can learn how to understand it and eradicate it from our life for good.

A person who possesses either anger or greed or even both of these traits (or any of the other socially unacceptable qualities we seem to have on this world), is not necessarily a bad person they are just here to learn what is deemed to be the negative aspect of that particular quality. We all, at some time or other, have to learn how to be unkind to our fellow earthly beings, whether they are human or otherwise. It may not be at this visit or even the next but there will come a time when these lessons need to be learned, just as we need to learn how to be kind and helpful.

Other tools we may possess while on earth are love, kindness, compassion and helpfulness. These are all qualities deemed to be socially acceptable but nevertheless they are just tools given to us to act out the various life experiences we have to endure during our stay on Earth.

Love is another emotional tool. Platonic love is the love of your family, friends and companions. This kind of love affects almost everybody; even the most evil of people love their Mums.

Let us now take a look at romantic love, the love between two people that helps to keep the planet populated.

How can love be a tool? Well love can be experienced in many ways. It would seem that love happens to most people during their lifetime and, for some, love can last throughout the whole of their life. They meet the right person and their love for that person will last until they die. Others may also love for the whole of their life but not just with one person. They may be romantically involved with many people throughout their life and love each one equally. There are also people who never find love but they never miss it either. In fact, not only do they not miss it, they are not even looking for it as love is not a tool they were given to learn from in this lifetime. An example of this type of person would be spinsters, bachelors, celibate priests, monks and nuns. There are many other people also who devote their lives to their work or religion, or have their own reasons for wishing to remain single. They are just ordinary people living out their lives, the same as you or I, but they are happy without the need to be romantically involved with others.

On the other hand, there are people who do not feel the need to give their love to others but will selfishly accept the love of others while giving nothing in return. Almost everybody on this world is affected by love in one way or another and will be learning to use this tool as part of the lessons they need during their stay on earth.

Have you ever thought why we are all so different throughout the world? The reason for this is that when people come down to this world they come down with different agendas, all lessons are slightly different from person to person and so the tools that are needed are varied. We may all come here with a full tool box but only the tools we need to use for this life are accessible to us.

Is it true that everybody will use different tools during their visits to the Earth?

The answer to this is 'no' as many of us can use the same tool to learn from because each tool has many attributes and can be either positive or negative. There are a given number of tools that are available for us to use on the Earth. We choose to come here because these tools and the Earth offer us the range of experiences that no other place can. The tools we use here are the baser kind of tools that give us the knowledge and experiences that we all need to learn from at the level we are at now. The lessons and experiences we learn here will refine our thinking and give us character and self-discipline which will help us to move on to finer things in the future.

I previously mentioned about the body being a tool but generally the thinking is, that "you are your body", or "your body is you", so it is easy to see the logic behind the belief that when your body dies you're dead. *This could not be further from the truth.* The fact is, your body is a tool and, although it is the most important piece of equipment you'll ever have while you are here on the Earth, the *real you* is the person inside it.

What are the attributes of your body? Well, its basic design is a head, two arms and two legs joined onto a torso which holds most of the vital organs that enable the whole body to function, and let's not forget the brain which is the computer. The brain sends out commands to other parts of your body to perform everyday functions like walking, bending, lifting, breathing and so on. We are all familiar with this bodily design and it enables us to move about freely and do the various tasks put before us throughout our stay on this planet.

What are the disadvantages of having a body like ours? One big problem with the design is that it damages easily and, when damaged, an immense amount of pain and discomfort can be felt. It is also prone to attack by various diseases and ailments that can cause organ failures putting the body under extreme distress and discomfort and, in some cases, even death. Our bodies have a very short lifespan compared to the lifespan of the Earth. Humans live on average for about 70-80 years. The age of the Earth is already roughly 4.5 billion years old.

Surely if we need to get the best out of our bodies while we are here, you would have thought the body we were given would have been strong enough, tough enough, and durable enough to be able to cope with all the hard work we are put through down here, and to be immune from the various diseases and ailments we are confronted with? Perhaps we should also have been given a longer lifespan to help us achieve everything we came down here to learn? Well, actually, our bodies have been made exactly as they are so that we are able to overcome, by experience, the problems of diseases, ailments, pain and discomfort as a part of the lessons we need to learn. We will always learn far more through hardship than we ever will through kindness or when everything is going well for us.

Let's look at hardship. It doesn't matter where you go on this world it's there, hardship. It's there amongst the poorer people of the world which is probably where you would expect it to be, it's there amongst the working classes, and it is also amongst the rich people of the world, where perhaps you would least expect it to be.

So what is this hardship? It comes to us in many guises. Many of us think of hardship as being without money but there are people suffering adversity in every walk of life. A wealthy person would have a different agenda than, say, that of a financially poorer person but with that different agenda comes just as many difficulties. Let us just look in general terms at these two scenarios.

A poorer person's main challenge would be to obtain enough money to feed themselves and their families, and then to make sure they had somewhere to live and enough clothes to wear. To fulfil these requirements they may have to work long hours for little pay and may even have to take on a second or third job to make ends meet. Being in this situation would bring with it many other challenges like over-tiredness, high levels of stress and low self-esteem leading, in turn, to physical and sometimes mental health problems. Having financial troubles also limits the opportunities that are available to them. Travelling abroad would definitely be out of the question and also taking on further education to broaden one's outlook. Without a decent education, the prospects of getting a better paid job would also be difficult, not least because of the lack of free time available. These are the conditions that a person who comes here to be fiscally challenged has to endure and this is a part of the education they will need, and which will enable them to rise above and beyond this world.

In fact all of us at some stage in our career, whether rich or poor, will have to learn how to overcome hardship and its associated lessons. Being poor is not an affliction bestowed upon a person as a punishment for their previous sin. It's just another one of the lessons that have to be learnt and is the reason why we come here. This world offers us the means we need to progress.

The wealthy also face their fair share of hardship as, believe it or not, being rich can bring about its own problems.

"So how hard is it to be wealthy?" Trust is a tough lesson to learn in this situation. Being able to trust others can be difficult. Are people really interested in you or is your money the attraction. A wealthy person will always be tested as they are in a privileged position on a world like this.

The following are two extreme examples:

1. Are you a person who likes to hoard money, just collecting wealth for the sake of it? Are you a greedy person who cares only for the acquisition of money and possessions and who has no thought of using it to help others?

2. Or are you a person who is overly generous, always thrusting your wealth upon others. Are you always giving help where it's not needed and has not been asked for just because you can, while hoping that it will put you in a good light with the boss man above and so ensuring that you get a good seat in Heaven when the time comes to leave?

Help others only when help is needed and when it's asked for but don't do it to excess. Let others have a chance to help themselves. Being poor or in need is not necessarily a permanent condition. For someone to work their way out of poverty by their own means may be the lesson they are here to learn. Be careful they are not deprived of achieving this goal.

It is not a sin to have money or possessions but it is wrong to be obsessed with acquiring them. These obsessions bring with them, amongst other things, greed, jealousy and even hatred. Money is just a tool which is loaned to us while we are on this Earth so that we are able to trade with each other. It is more convenient than bartering and it keeps the business of trading and making financial transactions flow smoothly throughout the world which is why it's called 'currency'.

I've talked quite a lot about hardship, pain, stress, doom and gloom but life is not all like that. Enjoyment is also a tool that is available for us to use and learn from. It's true that most of us live in a world where stress dominates. We always seem to be under some sort of pressure. It is also true that we learn quicker when presented with adverse conditions, which seem to kick-start us into action, but we also need to learn how to relax as well. This will also help us to cope more easily with the problems that are placed before us.

Employing the tool of enjoyment, no matter what our circumstances are, will make any difficult situation we are faced with a lot easier to handle. Life will always be hard here, that is just the nature of this world. The lessons we are here to learn at this level can be very cruel. On occasions, we may find it difficult to get started on our own when it comes down to learning a lesson we know will be unpleasant. We are able to sense this impending doom being thrust upon us through our intuition as we pick up our messages of guidance from either our Higher Self or Guides. We all need a little push now and then to force the situation and this will eventual give us no choice but to take the action needed.

If life was perfect, just one big holiday, where we all enjoyed only sunshine and laughter with no stress, heartache, or pain attached to it, who in their right mind would want to leave the party to learn something they didn't really want to? Would you? I don't think so.

If the lesson to be learnt involved a little discomfort or perhaps even a bit of pain with maybe some emotional problems thrown in for good measure, there would probably not be a lot of interest in learning them, even though the lesson would ultimately be to our advantage and future progress. Everyone would be far too busy having 'a good time'. That seems to be human nature.

Unfortunately life isn't a holiday. It is one big school term, where the lessons are hard and the days are long. So how do we learn to enjoy ourselves while we are suffering, how can we make things easier or a little more bearable? *We learn how to breathe properly and we learn to relax.*

Meditation is one way of relaxing your body. When meditating, even though our body completely relaxes, our mind is working hard. We are teaching it to focus so that we are able to take control over it and not let it control us. When we have control of our mind, we are able to handle stress better and apply our mind to the problems at hand, so making them easier to solve.

I will be looking further into the subjects of meditation and relaxation later in this book.

Looking on the positive side of things is also helpful. When we are relaxed and our mind is in positive mode, life will be more enjoyable. No matter what adversities come our way, we will handle them with ease. There are many positive tools in our tool box but unfortunately they are not used as much as they should be. Maybe it's because we like complaining so much!

Who is God?

This is not a book about religion. Religion is a completely different subject. Its concerns are more about teaching people to behave properly in society. It teaches its followers they should love God and their fellow beings and dispel all hatred from their lives. "Do unto others as you would have them do unto you."

"So who is God?" It is tempting to think that God is a kindly grandfather figure, with long white hair and flowing beard, someone who is looking over us at every moment seeing that we come to no harm. That's fine. There are many people who find comfort and security in that thought and also the thought that, when they die, they will go to Heaven and be safely seated by God's side.

This is a lovely metaphor; our whole life is mapped out for us. There is no need to push ourselves, no need to strive for achievement. We can just live out our seventy or eighty years on this world and then go straight to Heaven where we will live in bliss for eternity at God's side. Unless of course you are going the other way!

Ask yourself, what would be the point of coming to live on the Earth for seventy or eighty years? Do you know how long eternity is? This is your homework for tonight and I'm not being patronising here. Just take a little time out and give it some serious thought.

Living one life just doesn't make any sense. What would we do with all the achievements we've earned? What about all the failures we had, how would we put them right? What would we do with all the knowledge and wisdom we have acquired during our stay on Earth? We would have no reason to take either with us because in Heaven we should have copious amounts of both and everything that we would ever need will be there, right at our finger tips. Death will be one long holiday living alongside God.

If everybody had just one life and you were one of the countless people who were born crippled, blind or deaf, or perhaps were poor and living in squalid conditions and with sickness from being half starved, how would you feel when comparing your life with those who were born into wealthy families and had the best of everything and also the freedom to enjoy their lives to the full? *How fair, does that make God look?*

We think of God as being a kind, loving and just being, always wanting the best for his flock but, if you take the time to look around, even in the world's wealthiest places you will find poverty, sickness and injustice. So, if there is only one life for everyone here on Earth then that would put God in a very different light. He would not be the kind, loving and fair God that we read about in religious books. He would be deemed to be the Creator who does not care for the beings He created. It might even be the case that as He watches over us He may be enjoying the suffering that is going on down here on Earth, because there seems to be so much of it.

If there is just one life on Earth for us, we know that God would not let us suffer just for the sake of it, so there must be some other explanation for the things that are happening to us while we are here. The most likely reason that some people seem to suffer more than others is that everybody has more than one life on Earth. We all come here many times. We have to come back because there is so much to learn. It would be impossible for us to learn everything in one lifetime.

Our lifespan is very short and our mental capacity is such that it can only absorb small amounts of information at any one time. There are constant strains on our bodies which mean that they tire easily and have to rest frequently. We spend about a third of our lives sleeping and that's without taking into account the frequent rest breaks we take throughout the day while we are awake. Our bodies are not designed to last for a long time. Even if they were able to last longer, the amount of battering they receive from just living on this world is too much for them to survive for any appreciable time. They have a tendency to wear out fairly quickly when exposed to the elements of this world. Even though we are thought to be the top predator, there are still creatures that predate us, and this shortens our lives even more.

Even though seventy or eighty years seems a long time to us, it isn't. Take into account the time we spend sleeping, this equates to approximately a third of our lifetime and then there are the many rest breaks taken throughout the day. This means that the amount of time left to learn is perhaps only fifty per cent of our lifetime on Earth, this is about thirty five to forty years. Taking away the first sixteen years we spend growing up and learning how to become a socially acceptable adult, this now leaves us just twenty four to thirty nine years of actual learning time. Well, this is not *exactly* how it works, I'm just trying to make the point that, in real terms, our seventy or eighty years is not very long at all. So, in order to learn the vast amount of knowledge that is available to us, and thereby gaining the wisdom from that knowledge, it will take a very long time. Therefore we have to come to this world many times before we are able move on elsewhere and start the next phase of our existence.

God

We may never know who God is. God is so remote from us He probably doesn't even know we exist. I am not trying to be alarmist or upset anybody who gains comfort from believing that God is close-by but, the fact is, our universe is so vast and just one of many hundreds of other universes, some that are even more massive than our own.

There are so many stars and planets out there that we do not even have a number in our language to say how many that is, neither do we have the technological means to count that many. There is a God but we are not advanced enough to understand the concept of the true God.

Let us look at this in a slightly different way.

A managing director of a multi-national company in central London employs 950 staff in the London office but also has offices in cities all over the world, employing over 10,000 staff worldwide and this includes a very small office in Tashkent Asia with a staff of only 5, including the cleaner.

As you can imagine, the managing director is a very busy person, working all hours of the day and sometimes night. He delegates to his managers who, in turn, entrust work to their own staff. This forms an efficient chain of command through the company which contributes to its success. In order to keep a good relationship with his London staff, he makes a point of remembering as many of their names as possible and encourages his managers to do the same. This ensures that every person working in the building feels that they are appreciated and of value to the company. This policy works well in the London office but it would be very doubtful if he would know the name of the cleaner in the Tashkent office.

His manager at the Tashkent office would be responsible for the welfare of the staff at this branch of the company.

Now, how does God fit into this scenario? Does God really know who *we* are? Our situation is like that of the Tashkent cleaner above. God lives in a completely different realm to us. You can call it Heaven, or you can call it anything you like. It is not just a case of looking up to the sky and saying "When I die I hope I'll go to Heaven." It just doesn't work like that. The realm of God is so remote from us that we need to be much more advanced to get invited in. Even our spiritual body, our soul, is far too coarse to be able to live in the realm of God. We will have to become much, much more refined than we are now.

The God we worship, the God we pray to, the Lord God our Creator is just like our managing director. I'm not saying that he is God. What I'm saying is that the hierarchy is the same. Let us look at it like this.

Imagine you have a ladder, say, a mile high, and placed every twelve inches along the ladder there is a rung. Each rung represents a realm or dimension. We live close to the bottom of the ladder on the third rung up and this represents the third dimension. Our world, the Earth, is a three dimensional world that is in a three dimensional universe. God would be living in the dimension or realm right at the top of this ladder and *that* is how far away from God we are. He would know of our universe as He would know of every universe. He would also know that our universe is populated but as we are much too far down the ladder for Him to be able to guide us, He has helpers who look after everyone in the universe we live in. They are beings of a similar nature to ourselves but are from a little further up the ladder than we are.

These helpers are closer to us in terms of evolutionary progress and have gone through and conquered all the challenges that we are going through right now. They are also far better placed to help us directly, more so than God is, because our vibrations are far too coarse to be close to God.

One of the reasons for this is that our intelligence is extremely limited and we are also far too aggressive and have a very violent nature. You don't have to look at the warring nations of this world to see aggression and violence; it displays itself down every street in every town and every city. You can feel the stress and tension of people just by walking down these streets. Look how aggressive and impatient drivers can be! If you don't pull away from the traffic lights the split second they turn green, you'll get blasted by the horn of the driver behind you. If you look in your rear view mirror you can see the aggression in their eyes as they try to bully you into moving off faster.

I know that many people come here to learn to overcome this kind of behaviour and many other socially unacceptable behaviours but, until we are able to rise above these challenges and others that are placed before us, then there is little chance of our moving up the ladder of evolution and little chance of obtaining the higher vibrations needed to move us up to the next realm above.

If we are not able to evolve, then this will put the realm of God even further away from us than it is already. We need to climb a lot further up the ladder before God starts to recognise us and know who we are. The vibrations of our spiritual body need to be much higher and more refined than they are at the moment for this to happen. Everyone can achieve this goal by making more of an effort to learn the lessons that are put before us while here on Earth. If the effort is not made, then we will have to come back here and take the lessons that we didn't learn, again. Even climbing up to the next rung of the ladder will make a huge difference to our lives in terms of feeling comfortable with ourselves and others around us. We will have more responsibility but with less physical effort than is needed on this world. Even though God is so far away, we are never left on our own, there is always someone to watch over us and give us guidance when we need it.

Guides and helpers

So, who is it that watches over us then? Well firstly there are guides. These are not Red Indian Guides, Tibetan Lama Guides or some ancient Chinese Philosopher Guides—there just wouldn't be enough of them to go around if everybody had one!

The guides who watch over us and give us help throughout our lives are beings who have previously lived on this world, or worlds like this one. They have already gone through the challenges that we are going through and have learnt everything they can from being at the level that we are at now. They have moved on and no longer have to come back here lifetime after lifetime but, in order to give a little bit back for the help that they have received during their stay here, they have elected to stay in this realm for a while longer to help and guide us throughout our life. This is not only good for us but it also gives them the opportunity to put into use the skills they learned while they were here and this, in turn, will help them when they move on up the ladder to the next phase of their journey.

We are also watched over by our Higher Self. What do I mean by Higher Self? Our Higher Self is the main part of us. That is to say, we are a small part of our Higher Self which is the part that is sent to worlds like the Earth to gather information and experiences that are needed for the Higher Self to move further up its ladder of evolution. We are the spark of life that animates our physical body. We are the spiritual body or soul that resides inside our flesh body. If you find this hard to follow, then think of it in the following terms.

Suppose you had to explore the depth of the Pacific Ocean for scientific purposes. You work for a company which needs to find out more about the geological structure of the ocean floor and to see if it is possible to build a laboratory there for further exploration. It is obvious that you cannot go down there yourself because of the hostile environment you will encounter. The way to solve the problem is to send down a probe which has been fitted with scientific instruments and sensing equipment to enable it to explore the ocean floor and send back data to the company above.

This is much the same problem that your Higher Self has. It is unable to come down to this world or for that matter any other world in our universe, as it lives in a completely different realm to us where the vibrations are much higher than in this universe. There is also a difference in the time there compared to the time here. Although the Higher Self is unable to come here, it still needs to acquire the knowledge and experiences that the many worlds in our universe are able to offer. Even though our Higher Self is unable to come here in person, it still needs to find a way to obtain the knowledge that this universe has to offer and this is where we come in. It sends a small part of itself here. There is a ready supply of human bodies available here which just need the spark of life, us, put in them.

When it's time for us come to the Earth and enter the newly developing baby's body, we do so just before it is born, then we live out the rest of our time here acquiring the knowledge we need from the experiences we have here on Earth. Then when the lifespan of that human body is over, we leave the body here and return to a place that we think of as 'Heaven' but, in fact, it isn't.

While we are living here we are constantly sending back information to our Higher Self. We are also receiving guidance that will keep us on track and help us to reach the goals which we came down here to achieve. This may sound unbelievable, a bit far-fetched or even a bit of science fiction to most people. You may believe that using a human body like robots cannot be right, which is understandable, but if you think that the human body is *all* that matters then I can understand your concerns but this is not the case.

Our physical body is a tool provided for us to use while living on this world and without it we would not be able to carry out the tasks which we came down here for. I know this may come as a bit of a shock but it's true. When we have finished with our human body we leave it here where it will be either cremated or buried but, either way, it is unable to function anymore. It is past its best before date.

The human body can be thought of as a costume that an actor would wear while acting out a part. The actor would wear this costume during the performance then when the show is over he would discard it and go back to his or her real life. The human body represents this costume. It has a definite lifespan of about seventy five to eighty years on average and when it reaches its designated age it dies but you, the spark of life inside, lives on. You do not die when your body does, you stay very much alive. The body that you are using in this life, or any other life on Earth for that matter, is provided especially for you. It would be useless and unable to function at all if you had not occupied it. It is a purpose-made item constructed solely for the job of giving you everything that you require to make your life on Earth, this time around, a successful one.

Prayers

So, who do we pray to if God doesn't know who we are? Is there any use in praying if there is nobody there to listen to our prayers? Well, it is always good to pray. Not only does it help us recognise the fact that sometimes we need help but it is also helps to relieve any stress we are under. The very fact that we ask for help not just for ourselves, but for others also, is an uplifting and feel-good thing to do. It gives us hope that some of our worries and uncertainties may be lifted and also that other people may benefit from our prayers as well.

Ok, so if we don't pray to God then who do we pray to? Well, this may come as a bit of a surprise but *we actually pray to ourselves*. What is the use of praying to ourselves if we are the ones who need the help? How on earth is that going to work? A lot of prayers are calls for help. "Please help me out of this situation; help me to help others; help me to stay on the right path so that I will go to Heaven". Praying does not necessarily have to be a religious experience. A prayer can simply be a question and all of our prayers and questions are directed to our Higher Self. If a question is relevant to our stay on Earth and is of a *need to know* nature, then you will receive an answer. If a prayer or question is of a *want to know* nature and is not necessarily relevant to our stay on Earth, then we probably will not receive an answer.

If we send prayers for others to help them to overcome whatever problem they have, no matter how much feeling we put into it and no matter how sorry we feel for that person and their suffering, we are still only praying to ourselves. It may be the case that the person we are praying for has come to this Earth in order to take on the particular suffering they are going through as a life lesson, in which case our prayers will not be answered. It is wrong to pray aimlessly without knowing the full circumstances of the person we are sending prayers too. We can never know what lessons other people are here to learn. We should be more concerned with our *own* life and the lessons that *we* are here to learn!

Your conscience

Messages are transmitted between a person and their Higher Self at all times. An in-coming message is received by the subconscious mind and is then relayed to another part of the brain. This message is recognised by the part of the brain that helps us to decide whether or not to take action and, if so, what action is necessary—this is our conscious mind.

For example, let's say that 'John' is planning to rob a bank. He gets together all the tools needed to carry out the job and one of his accomplices, Freddie, gets out a gun and puts it with the rest of the tools. John sees the gun and immediately feels uneasy about taking it with them. He gives the gun back to Freddie telling him it is not needed. Although John is quite happy to rob a bank, his conscience is telling him not to take the gun. He is a thief in this life, not a killer.

So what is happening here? John is not worried about stealing money from banks but carrying a gun to kill is not one of the lessons he needs to learn, so his Higher Self sends him a message "No Guns." When John receives this message by way of his conscience, it makes him feel uneasy so he gives the gun back. Part of his training in this life is to experience what happens around him when he steals from others. He is learning how it affects other people and also how it will affect him. John's Higher Self is giving him guidance and stopping him from straying too far from the path that he has chosen to take in this life. Killing would have put him on an entirely different path.

The lesson to learn here is, if a person ignores the guidance they are given and they stray too far off their path in this life, they will have to come back here to learn it over again. Always be guided by your conscience. By listening to what your mind is telling you, you will become more intuitive. The voice may be a little quiet at first but if you learn to listen and recognise that there *is* a voice there, it will become louder and clearer. It will also help to make it easier for you to keep to the path you have chosen in this life.

Please note: The voice of guidance comes to you from your Higher Self and not from God. As previously stated, we do not have the understanding in this realm to know who God is, and He is unable to come down to our level to let us know who He is.

Why do we have to live on Earth?

It's all very well explaining why we are on this world and what we have to do while we are here, but how do we get here? We now know that we are a small part of our Higher Self that comes down and enters the human body before it is born. So how does this happen?

Well, it is not just a case of picking any old body to wear and hope that it all works out for the best. Coming to live on the Earth can take many years of planning and preparation and there must be a reason why we need to come here. Your Higher Self will know the reason and will identify the lessons that need to be learnt. Discussions will then take place with guides and helpers, who are experienced in such matters, as to the best way of going about things.

To begin with there will be a search for suitable parents, followed by many meetings between the prospective parents, the helpers and the person who will occupy their child's body. Are the chosen parents living in the right situation? Are their vibrations compatible with the frequency of the person that they will be bringing up as their child? Do they live in a country that will afford their new child the best living conditions and opportunities necessary for the lessons that the child needs to learn. Will the parents be happy to bring up this child and help it achieve the goals necessary to make his or her journey through life a successful one?

So, there are many things that need to be taken into consideration. It is the same for everyone. Your Higher Self is unable to come to a world like the Earth because the environment is too hostile, and also the universal vibrations are too low. It would be like a human being trying to live in the ocean without any breathing apparatus. Our Higher Self, however, is able to send a small part of itself here to live inside a machine that is more suited to the earthly environment, the human body. The soul or spirit is able to reduce its vibrations to an acceptable level of that of the human body and live in a state of symbiosis for a short while. The human body is designed to hold the soul or spirit inside it. In fact the body is unable to function without the soul or spirit. Also, the soul is unable to stay on the Earth without being connected to the body so the symbiotic relationship between the two works out quite well. Although the partnership between the soul and the body works well, we certainly make it difficult sometimes for the partnership to always run smoothly.

Vices

I am of course referring to the abuse that we put our body through. Alcohol is probably the biggest offender today. This is because it is socially acceptable to have a drink while in the company of others. Alcohol taken in small or moderate amounts every once in a while does little harm to the body or the soul but, when taken frequently and in large amounts, it creates all sorts of problems not only for the body but also for the soul. We all know about the damage alcohol does to the various organs in the body but nobody mentions the damage it does to the soul.

When alcohol is drunk in copious amounts, leaving a person incapable of functioning properly, it causes the body's vibrational frequency to fall so low that the soul is driven out of the body, although it is still attached by way of the Silver Chord. It will not be able to return until the person sobers up and the vibrational frequency returns back to its normal level. The saying that he was "out of his head" is very true. When a person is very drunk the soul leaves the body to cope with its situation the best it can. This is why a drunken person will find it difficult to walk, balance or have any co-ordination at all. Even remembering things that happened while under the influence will also be difficult. You can relate this to a computer that has had its hard drive removed. It is still a computer but is unable to function properly because one of the key parts has been taken away. It becomes incapable of holding any processed information whatsoever. It is just a machine that will hum a little when plugged in, similar to that of a drunk sitting on a park bench.

Taking un-prescribed drugs is also an abuse on the body and soul. It is not as wide-spread as alcohol abuse because it isn't accepted in everyday society like alcohol, nevertheless there are many people in the world who are affected by drug addiction. Being addicted to drugs or alcohol will affect a person's life in many ways but the most serious effect of all is that of an early death for the person who cannot fight off the addiction. It is serious because it is a violation of Universal Law and is regarded as a self-inflicted death, in other words, suicide. I will talk about suicide later in this book.

Smoking is also an addiction but one that may be a little easier to stop. It is becoming less acceptable to smoke in the company of others because of the passive smoking issue and the unpleasant odour that is attached to a person who smokes.

The same rule applies to someone who dies of a smoking-related illness earlier than the allotted time they were given. If they are aware that their actions will shorten their lives then they will be held responsible for cutting down the time they were given to complete their tasks on Earth. Their death will therefore be regarded as suicide. So, it is best to leave these three vices alone, unless they are a part of your life lesson of course.

Working on this world

Once again, we will be working with guides, helpers and prospective parents who will arrange for us to come and live on this Earth so that we can learn from the many experiences that are on offer here.

Why do we need to learn these lessons?

Surely there must be a very good reason for us to want to come to a place that we know will only give us nothing but grief. It is the poorer countries of the world that appear to suffer the most. We hear on a daily basis about the poverty, harsh weather conditions, crop failure, hunger, war, over-population and many other natural disasters that happen in these parts of the world.

The wealthier parts of the world also have their fair share of problems. They may not be quite as physically extreme as some of the poorer countries of the world, or so it would seem at first glance, but the problems of the wealthy are of a different kind. They are a little more subtle but nevertheless they still cause untold grief and unhappiness.

People living in western societies tend to suffer in silence while their problems niggle away in the background getting progressively worse. Because these problems are quite subtle, they are not confronted head-on but pushed aside and will eventually cause tension within the body. This in turn will bring on stress which, if not dealt with, can lead to physical illness along with mental problems. It is disorders like these that can affect some people to such an extent that they are unable to see a way out of their problems. It is this feeling of desperation that will eventually lead them to depression and then even to suicide.

So why do we come here? It's those lessons again. This world offers our Higher Self exactly what it needs in order to progress.

When we were attending school, we didn't go into the gym to learn maths or onto the school football pitch to learn woodwork or biology. We went to the appropriate classrooms. This world is the appropriate classroom for our Higher Self. It is the ideal learning place that never allows us to get too comfortable. There is always something to go wrong, always a challenge to be faced or a decision to be made. We can never rest on our laurels for long. We are constantly pushed a little further, a little harder and continually onwards. Time is always short so we have to make the most of our stay here.

As I have said previously, we are never sent here to suffer more than we can cope with. We are always given the right tools to work with and there is always guidance at hand when it is needed. We are never asked to take on more tasks or learn more lessons that we came here for, although sometimes we may think we are 'hard done by', this is usually because we are feeling a little sorry for ourselves.

The world itself can present us with all sorts of challenges. Unpredictable weather conditions, earthquakes, volcanoes and tsunamis are all capable of causing extreme life-changing experiences for the unfortunate people affected by them. Worldwide, diseases kill and maim millions of people every year. An asteroid crashing through the earth's atmosphere can cause world-changing events. The next event may be the one that makes the human race extinct, thereby preparing the Earth to be inhabited by a new race of people. So, there are many things happening on our world all the time making it an ideal place to learn from. It is just unfortunate that most of our learning is achieved through suffering and hardship. As we climb further up the ladder of evolution our lessons will be just as demanding as they are now, the difference however, will be marked by the responsibilities that we will have to undertake, both for ourselves and others who are as yet unable to make their own decisions. Bearing responsibility for others is harder than any of the heavy physical work that we do here on this world.

When we die and leave this world, after a period of recovery, we will not necessarily come back here straight away, if at all. Even so, there is still much to do and much to learn even when we are not on this world. Our brief visits to the Earth, and to other worlds also, are not our true lives. They are just mere excursions of learning, much the same as we would enrol in a college course or take a break from work to go to university to increase our qualifications. We do not stay at college or at university forever, we leave when we have finished the course and then incorporate what we have learnt into our real lives so that we can move on.

The Earth is the place we call 'home' but it is not our real home, it is a place manufactured for the purpose that it will be used. We on Earth also manufacture purpose-made facilities such as schools, hospitals, office blocks and factories but we don't live in them, they are built for their own specific purposes.

It is the same with the Earth, our galaxy and all galaxies. The same applies to the whole universe and everything it contains. Everything that we understand as being real and natural is just manufactured. It is made for a specific use, not just for us. We are not the centre of importance in our universe. There are many different races on countless planets in our universe, all of them are manufactured the same as us. All of them are living on planets made for the purpose and all of them are living out their allotted lifespan and then moving on, the same as us. If we care to look, we can see this manufacturing process in progress. It is happening all the time, just above our heads.

Responsibility

So, the more we move away from the physical way of life of the Earth, where the only thoughts of the people occupying it are of a material nature, the more responsibility we seem to get.

What do I mean by responsibility? Well, responsibility on Earth revolves mostly around acquiring money and material possessions. For example:

The Managing Director of a company will have the responsibility to ensure that the company produces a good profit at the end of each year. In order for this to happen he or she will keep pressure on their managers at all times even when profits are high. The managers are responsible to the directors and the company for maintaining the high standard of production that will help to maintain a high annual profit so, they in turn, have to encourage the manual workers whose responsibility it is to manufacture the company products as quickly as possible.

I realise that this is a generalisation, and that there are exceptions but, on the whole, this is how responsibility in a capitalist society works, always chasing a higher profit and then holding others responsible when no profit is made. Even some Communist countries have modified the structure of their industries to manufacture and flood the world with their own products. Their belief system is changing as their wealth increases and they are now leaning more towards the capitalist's way of doing things, more so than ever before.

When we move away from the system of responsibility that applies here on Earth, then the system of responsibility changes radically. We take on a lot more responsibility when we leave this world but the work that we do will not be for financial gain.

We will take on the responsibility of helping those who have less understanding than that of ourselves and also of those who are new to this realm and don't know their way around yet. It can be quite bewildering being the 'new kids on the block' and not knowing what is right from wrong or how to behave in the different societies of this world. With no prior knowledge of this realm these are people are unable to make their own decisions and have to rely on others for help and guidance.

Can you remember how nervous you were when you left your primary school and moved up to the comprehensive or high school? The school building seemed so big, the school desk and chair were so tall that your feet couldn't touch the floor, and the new school procedures were confusing for you compared to your previous school. You may have felt totally out of place and completely out of your comfort zone but, after a while, your confidence built up slowly and you began to feel that you were starting to fit in. You made new friends and where able to find your way around a little better so your confidence grew even more. Having attended the school for a few years, you learnt many academic lessons and also many life lessons, you were able then to be in a position to help new arrivals coming into the school for the first time and who were as frightened and alone as you once were.

This is exactly the same situation that people will find themselves in when they come to this realm for the first time. When they arrive here everything is so completely alien to them. They need to spend some time acclimatising to their new situation while being shown by the helpers just how things work around here. At this point they are totally unable to make even the simplest of decisions let alone know how to plan their own future. When they arrive here they have no experience of appropriate behaviour or how to acquire the knowledge and wisdom needed to progress further. They are completely reliant on their helpers who have elected to stay in this realm a little longer rather than move straight on to the next one. Helpers are people who have been in this realm for a very long time and have learnt from experiencing all that has been on offer to them, although, they feel they could still benefit by staying here a little longer to assist others.

There are many ways in which these helpers can share their knowledge and experience to help others. I have already mentioned a little about those who have come here for the first time feeling bewildered and frightened because the realm they have just left is so vastly different to this one. Before the new arrivals are sent down to worlds like the Earth, they are given a little time to settle in, so to speak, and recover from their ordeals. It is then that the helpers will bring them down to a level which is between the physical worlds and so called spiritual realm, this level is called the Astral Plane.

The Astral Plane is an area that lies between physical worlds like the Earth and the spiritual realm (which is known as Heaven according to some religions). It is a place where the vibrational frequencies are much higher than that of the Earth, so our physical body is unable to go there. The Astral Plane is the place where our spiritual body can meet other spiritual people, like guides and helpers who have come from the spiritual realm down to the Astral Plane to assist others face to face.

The Astral Plane is also the place where the spiritual body of a person from the Earth can meet deceased relatives and friends who have passed on from Earth and now live in the spiritual realm. We are able to meet them when we are sleeping and our spiritual body leaves the physical body. This type of visitation is called astral travelling or an 'out of body' experience. Our physical body needs to have frequent rest periods but our spiritual body doesn't need to rest so can leave the physical body while it sleeps.

When a newcomer is taken to the Astral Plane the person is looked after by guides and helpers who decide for the person the type of lessons they will need to learn during their first visits to the Earth, or any other suitable world in this universe. Suitable parents will have to be found to enable this person to be born on Earth. This being their first time here, they will need plenty of help and guidance during their stay. Their guides and helpers will be in constant touch with them throughout their stay here and will have many meetings on the Astral Plane, which will take place while the physical body is asleep.

Another role of the helper is to look after people when their allotted lifespan is over and they die, that is, when their physical body dies. They may be suffering from severe trauma, especially if their life on Earth was a particularly long and difficult one. Sometimes the lessons we need to learn while we are here can be very hard indeed and we may require the help and specialist care of someone who has encountered, and overcome, similar conditions during their own stay on Earth.

The type of work that helpers undertake can be very demanding and requires a high level of responsibility. There are millions of people dying every day who require assistance from helpers when they return to the realm they call 'home'. Likewise there are millions of people being born every day and a large number of these people also require assistance from helpers. Helpers do not get paid for the work they do, their reward is the satisfaction they receive from the help they give. The experience of giving help will also hold them in good stead when it's time for them to move on to the next stage of their lives.

If a helper has a particular skill which they have specialised in while studying on their many visits to the Earth, they will then be able to assist the guide who is looking after the person who needs to learn this particular skill. Everybody on Earth will have many guides and helpers throughout their lifetime, each one giving their help just when the time is right. Most people will never see or be aware of their helpers or guides while they are living here. It is only when we develop our intuitive senses that we will become aware of the existence of the guides and helpers and ultimately our Higher Self.

Help and guidance

Well, as I have previously stated, when we come down to this world we are never alone. We have guides and helpers who look after us during our frequent visits here. They make sure that we stay on the path that was chosen for us when preparations were made for us to come to this world. These guides and helpers are also taking direction from our Higher Self who knows exactly what we need to experience while we are here.

Guides no longer reside in this realm as their physical vibrations are of a much higher frequency than that of the Earth or even this universe. This makes them incompatible and prevents them from coming directly down to this world. To be able to come to this world would mean that they would have to be re-born into an earthly body and make their vibrational frequency lower and more compatible with that of the Earth's frequency. They would then need to spend time growing to adulthood before they were able to give their guidance. Apart from being time-consuming and impractical, this measure could increase the world population by perhaps more than five-fold and humans, being naturally sceptical, probably wouldn't believe a single word of guidance they were given anyway. Most people would be just drifting along aimlessly without any clue as to what they were supposed to be doing.

Fortunately it doesn't work like that. We are guided from a higher realm where messages sent to us are received by intuition and also via the subconscious mind.

There are many people who are completely unaware of this process, they do not hear or see any messages sent to them or even notice the guidance they are given. It would seem that they are drifting along in this life without any guidance at all but this is not so. The decisions they should be making for themselves are made for them by their guides and helpers, and any lessons left unlearnt will be given to them again in a future life here on Earth.

There are also many people who are aware of intuition and the subconscious mind but do not act upon the guidance they are given as they are unable to understand what it is they are hearing. The reason for this is that the messages being sent are very quiet and can easily be overlooked or ignored. Most people are unable to control what thoughts come into their minds because their minds are always busy and cluttered with unwanted thoughts. Our brains are being bombarded by random thoughts and outside stimuli at all times, so the help and guidance that is given just gets muddled up with everything else and goes unnoticed.

Why isn't the guidance we are given, sent to us so that we can hear it clearly? This is a valid question but, if you were to give it some serious thought, you would see that if everything was spelt out to us every step of the way then we would not be learning through our own experiences. We would not be overcoming the challenges given to us, ourselves. We receive guidance, not the answers.

When students are sitting an examination they are given the exam papers containing the questions but if the examiner talked them through the questions and so helping them to achieve the answers, instead of letting them get on with the exam by themselves, the achievement of passing the exam would be meaningless.

The same applies to receiving guidance and intuitive messages from our Higher Self, guides and helpers. The messages are only given when they are needed, therefore if a person is going through a difficult period in their life or maybe they have reach an impasse which they are unable to overcome, then guidance is given but they will have to pay attention to their thoughts. If they do not, they may miss important information being sent to them which will help them to overcome their problems and ultimately give them the opportunity to move on.

There are some people who are able to hear, and recognise, messages of guidance and direction without any trouble at all. The people with this ability are those who have been around this realm for quite a while and have learnt and experienced almost everything that this realm has to offer, therefore it will soon be time for them to move on. Their physical vibrations have reached a much higher frequency than that of others who are just starting out or those who are only halfway through their journey in this realm.

People with a high vibrational frequency will find themselves incompatible with others of a lower frequency. When two people meet and the frequencies of each are very different, they will feel uncomfortable when in each other's company and will probably never be friends or have any kind of relationship together. This does not mean that the person with a higher frequency is any better than the person with the lower frequency. It just indicates that the person with the higher frequency has been around a little longer and it will soon be time for them to leave this realm and move on in their life.

The Earth and other planets in this universe can only accept beings within its own frequency range. Anybody outside this frequency with either a higher or lower range will find it impossible to live here. It would be the same as bringing ice into a room where the temperature is 25 degrees Celsius; it would not be able to stay in the room as ice because the room would be too warm.

When a person's vibrational frequency starts to rise beyond the range of this realm, it is an indication that they will soon be unable to live in this three dimensional universe and will have to move on to a different place where the frequencies are more compatible with their own. It is through this process that a person is able to progress, moving from one realm to another, always learning, always climbing the ladder of evolution. Every time we move on to a different realm then our vibrational frequency will increase and will keep increasing as we move up through the dimensions. We will eventually reach a point when we will no longer need to use physical bodies to progress or to go through the life and death cycle of finding parents, being born and then dying. Our spiritual bodies will have a high enough frequency to carry on learning just as they are.

Breathing and Meditation = Relaxation

There are many dimensions that we will need to visit to carry on our quest for learning. At this particular moment, we are just at the beginning of our journey. We think we know so much but even now we are only aware of one dimension, the one we are currently living in, our universe.

Quite frankly, we know very little about this universe because we are so small and have limited technology. We are able to look out into the great expanses of our universe with our large modern telescopes and almost see the bigger picture but unfortunately we are missing the smaller detail. We do not have the means to see the enormous variety of life out there or the unlimited amount of abundance that is available to us. "Why?" Because we are too busy bickering amongst ourselves. If everybody on this world were to pull together and make an effort to move forward in the same direction, instead of fighting and arguing with each other, then our progress would be such that the universe would be our oyster. While we have greed, anger, jealousy and a need to always be the one that is right, our progress will always be slow. If we had a ladder ten kilometres high and each rung represented a dimension, then we would be the third rung from the bottom. That's a sobering thought.

We will always be physically limited by how much we can learn while we are on this world. Being reliant on technological advancement to move us forward is always going to be a slow process because of the nature of human beings and, despite the large population of this world, there are surprisingly very few people who are directly in the forefront of technological advancement. Yet, there are other ways to move forward.

If we were to look inside ourselves we would find out so much more and our world would open up to all sorts of new and exciting life-changing discoveries. So what do I mean by looking inside ourselves?

Well, there are many ways that we are able to regain control of our thoughts and so change the way that we think. It is not very often that the average person is able to sit down, relax and completely switch off from the noise and bustle of everyday life. The way many people relax is by putting their feet up and watching the television or perhaps they will read a book or a newspaper, which is fine, but that is *not* relaxing. Relaxing is not doing any of those things, true relaxing is doing the complete opposite.

It is only when we learn to relax properly that our mind becomes quiet. Having a quiet mind means that there are no random or unwanted thoughts intruding into it. So, with a clear mind and a body that is in a relaxed state, we are able to start to look inside ourselves.

The key to real relaxation is knowing how to breathe correctly. The suck and blow technique, that most people seem to use, is not the correct way to breathe. It will keep them alive but it will not help their health or keep them in a relaxed or stress-free state, either physically or mentally. It is worth learning how to breathe properly if only to be able to handle stressful situations in a peaceful and more controlled way.

If everybody breathed correctly, life could be open to all sorts of changes and benefits. This world would be a more relaxed and pleasant place to live in. Breathing properly will help your mind and body to be more relaxed. A relaxed mind and body carries an air of peace about it so-much-so that your whole body's demeanour changes. A relaxed and peaceful person is a pleasant person to be with.

Being able to relax the body is a difficult thing to do; breathing correctly is the first step. When breathing, many people only use the top part of their lungs (*top or shallow breathing*). They pull the diaphragm in when they inhale so restricting the intake of air to the top half of their lungs. This has the following two effects:

1.   A person who is top breathing will have to breathe far more often than a person who is using the whole of

their lungs. The reason for this is that they are only taking in half of the oxygen required by their body from a single breath.

2.   The person's shoulders rise every time they inhale thereby bringing unnecessary tension to the shoulders and neck. Top breathing does not promote relaxation in fact it does the complete opposite. When a person has to breathe more often than necessary and also continually lift and drop their shoulders with every breath, it can only promote stress and anxiety within their body and mind.

Breathing correctly

Breathing correctly is simple but not easy to do, especially if you have spent most of your life breathing incorrectly. It is simple because all you have to do is inhale, fill your lungs completely and then exhale emptying your lungs completely. Things start to get difficult when it is realised that you will have to breathe like this all the time and it will also have to be done by breathing through your nose.

There are many people who always breathe through their mouth. This is fine when breathing out but when a person inhales this way, the air they are taking in has not been filtered nor has it had its temperature controlled. The air just goes straight into their lungs carrying with it any dirt, dust or other particles that happen to be floating near the mouth at the time of inhalation. It is possible that, when breathing like this, it could be one of the major causes of respiratory problems, especially if a person were to breathe like this all the time.

So, learning to breathe through our noses at all times is the first thing we need to do. Obviously we would not breathe this way while running or doing hard physical exercise but the normal everyday breathing that we do to keep ourselves alive should be done by breathing through the nose. As we inhale, the diaphragm, which is positioned in the front centre of the body just below the rib cage, will push out allowing air to get down to the bottom of the lungs. When we exhale, the diaphragm should pull back as the air gets pushed out of our lungs. When breathing like this, it should be done without forcing the air into our lungs. By breathing gently in and gently out, our breathing will slow down, the shoulders will stop going up and down, and the urgency to gulp in another lungful of air will disappear because just one normal slow breath will be sufficient to give our body all the oxygen it needs.

Breathing is an automatic process. We don't have to think about breathing in or breathing out, it just happens. When our body has used up the oxygen which it has just breathed in, the carbon dioxide content of the lungs will start to rise forcing our body to breathe out, so we are then able to breathe back in again. This operation is handled by the subconscious mind. When we have learnt to do correct breathing consciously, we will then have to train our body to stop using the incorrect breathing pattern and start using the correct breathing pattern.

This will require quite a lot of effort on our part to begin with but it is well worth doing as the benefits far outweigh the effort. To do this we will need to focus on how we are breathing several times during the course of day. If we find that we are not breathing properly then we need to change this by starting to use the correct breathing pattern that we have just learnt (above) and, over a short period of time, our body will get used to the idea of how we want it to breathe and it will then start to use the correct breathing pattern automatically.

Once the correct breathing pattern is being used automatically, the body will start to relax naturally and will always stay fairly relaxed whether we are moving or remaining still. When this happens it will then be time for us to take the next step and work on quietening the mind.

The Mind

Almost everybody seems to have an over-active mind that is always 'on the go'. It seems impossible to have a moment of peace or any quiet time at all. In this situation, the mind just keeps absorbing thought after thought until it has so much information that it has to be stored away without any chance of it being sorted. There is just too much data coming in. Why is this?

Well, the brain has a tremendous capacity for processing data. We have a computer inside our head that is far more powerful than any computer that man has built to date. Most of the information that is received by the brain is repetitive or unimportant data which it finds impossible to stop receiving. It is constantly being flooded with what we could call "junk mail".

The sheer quantity of unwanted 'data' that we receive can cause stress within our mind and will eventually manifest itself throughout the body. Breathing correctly will help us to relax, thereby quietening the mind which, in turn, will alleviate the effect of stress and stress-related illnesses within the body.

Fortunately, even under the influence of stress, the functions of all the important organs in our body carry on working; they are driven automatically by the subconscious mind. The replacement of skin layers and also the immune system are among many of the functions that our brain has been programmed to look after. Although we don't have to think about operation of our organs, they can still be affected when we are suffering from stress.

The bodily functions that are *not* automatic are the ones that we have to think about operating and are used for the more mundane tasks that have to be performed e.g. moving around, carrying out simple physical tasks and being free to make our own decisions. All functions in our charge are under the control of our conscious mind and are fairly simple operations, we are able to carry these out by using our free-will although, they still demand a great deal of concentration on our part. When the mind is constantly being bombarded with information, our decision-making and concentration can be affected, thereby placing a great deal of stress on the body. This stress can cause a number of unpleasant physical side effects and, if not taken seriously, may lead to a physical or even a mental breakdown.

Calming the Mind

The brain, although as powerful as it is, can be trained. If a person wants to make themselves fit or strengthen up their body, they will go down to the local gym to lift weights or do exercises. By continually doing a repetitious set of exercises, a person will be able to build up the strength and fitness within their body. It is the same for the brain. If the brain is given a set of repetitive thoughts to focus on, it will after a while, stop accepting random unwanted thoughts. This will free up the mind from being cluttered and promote empty spaces and quiet moments that can be filled with our own positive thoughts, thoughts that will be of more benefit to us than the clutter. This is Meditation.

Meditation is extremely beneficial in many ways. To be able to focus our mind on a single thought without any distractions creeping in, will give our mind the ability to maintain its concentration no matter what thought the focus is on. By understanding this, it will also become apparent that meditation is a most powerful tool for the development of our mind especially when practised regularly.

It will take a little while but if meditation is practised every day it will stimulate our powers of contemplation (*contemplation is the observation or study of a matter in depth*). Contemplation is very useful when there is a problem to solve or when we need to seriously consider the answer to any questions that have been asked or, indeed, when it is necessary to concentrate at length to understand a subject more fully. Contemplation enables us to give our full attention to any situation that may arise during our life that demands our total concentration. It also enables us to look at the situation at hand from every angle, thereby giving the best chance of a solution to a problem or to understand the right answer to a question we have asked.

There are many other benefits derived from the practise of regular meditation. Relaxation, for example, can be difficult to achieve but I have found that the most effective way of relaxing is through regular meditation. By maintaining the focus of the meditation for about twenty to thirty minutes per session, the body will relax so completely that all physical tension within our body will gradually and gently disappear. The feet, legs, hands and arms will feel as if they are no longer part of us. It can be quite alarming when this happens for the first time but when it happens more regularly it will become a satisfying part of our meditation.

Relaxing the body may take just a little longer but, when we achieve total relaxation throughout our meditation, we will find that our breathing rate slows down so much that it is almost undetectable. The heart rate also slows, so the circulation of blood around the body is reduced. The organs within our body also become relaxed and slow down, thereby helping us to achieve total relaxation.

Stress plays a major part in most people's lives. There are some people who thrive on stress and stressful situations. They need that little buzz of adrenalin to be able to handle what might be to most people, difficult situations. There are many people who work in jobs where there are difficult challenges and where major decisions need to be made on a daily basis. Dealing with stress in this way is alright for a short period but to live this way over a long period of time can only be detrimental to one's health.

One of the major benefits of practising meditation comes from the ability it gives one to handle stress. Through meditation we are able to tackle any stressful events that arise with ease. This is due to the relaxed disposition and confidence we will have gained through meditation. Being able to conquer stress easily takes the strain off our body so that our character changes from one of anguish to one of peace and tranquillity. Being able to remain in this state of mind, where clarity of thought and openness is always with us, will help us to redeem any situation we find ourselves in, quickly and calmly, leaving us unflustered and ready for the next challenge that will undoubtedly come our way.

Although meditation is effective when being done on a regular basis, it does not prevent stress from occurring in one's life.

There will always be stressful situations in life; it's the way life is on this planet. Meditation will help you to handle stress easier but meditation will only work when it is being practised. You cannot store up meditation and use its effectiveness as and when needed—if you don't do it, it doesn't work.

My recommendation is that everybody should be taught to meditate. It doesn't matter what style or technique of meditation you choose to learn, they all lead to the same place. The practice of meditation is life-changing. Living on this planet would be a joy if everybody were to practise the art of meditation. The world itself will not change, there will always be natural disasters, extreme weather conditions and discomfort here but the people living on this world will change. It is the people that make this world what it is and at the moment, in most cases, it is not a nice place to be.

Quite simply, if you would like your life to change and would like to have peace of mind with an understanding of where you are going on this world then learn to meditate. If you do not want these things then don't meditate.

It is only a pipe dream and a waste of energy to think that this world could be any different than it is. It has been manufactured for a purpose. This world is a place of learning, a school that has been designed to test and prove the beings that live on it, whether they are humans or not. It gives the right conditions necessary for all of its occupants to learn from. There is a wide variety of beings living here with different abilities and who are at different stages of their evolution. The vast and varied conditions we have here, makes this an ideal place to learn from. It gives everyone the chance to learn the lessons that are needed and a chance for all to move on in their lives. This world is unable to change but the beings on it *are* able to change.

I know that I have already mentioned in a previous chapter that this is a place where we all come to learn, and I shall probably mention it again in future chapters, but I feel that it is important that everybody reading this should understand how it really is. We all have the ability to choose whether we learn our pre-arranged lessons with gratitude, enthusiasm and with a sense of joy that we have been given the chance to improve ourselves. Or, we could go through life moaning and being a victim. Yes, we really do have that choice.

I have talked a great deal about meditation and the benefits of practising it outside of this book. So how is it done? What are the requirements and where do I start?

Those who do not understand meditation or its purpose would have you believe that it is strange or even mystical and that only the spiritual amongst us can practise it. This is not true. There is nothing mystical about meditation and it is available and beneficial to everyone.

There are many websites on the Internet that sell 'Learn to Meditate' CDs. Buddhist websites seem to be a good source of information for meditation although I would not necessarily recommend that CDs are the best way to learn meditation. They can be quite expensive and not really the best method of learning.

Meditation courses are also available and again there are many to choose from on the Internet if that is the way you choose to learn.

A better way to learn meditation, and one which I fully endorse, is to go to your local Buddhist centre or temple where they hold meditation classes. You will find that they are mostly free of charge to all. By attending a live class, there will always be someone at hand to help and guide you if you have any difficulties. You don't have to be a Buddhist to attend these classes and they won't try to recruit you. It is a good way to get started into meditation and you will get the help and guidance if it is needed. It will give you a good foundation to start with and also help you on your journey into meditation.

The requirements to meditate are minimal. In fact the only thing that is really needed is determination, patience and an ability to stay with it even when things aren't going as expected.

So, how do we meditate?

There are many meditation techniques and styles around. It doesn't really matter at this stage which one you start with, although for a beginner it is better to start off by using a simple technique. When you start to get results coming through, and you feel that you are ready to progress further, you can move on to other styles of meditation.

Let me give you an example of Meditation. This is called "Watching the Breath".

Sit in a comfortable position, either on a chair, or cross-legged on the floor with a cushion or, if you have one, use a meditation stool. It is not important what you sit on just as long as your back is straight but don't try to force your back straight if it won't straighten naturally. If, for instance, you have a curvature of the spine then you will not be able to straighten your back so just sit as upright as you can but in a position comfortable for yourself. If you are sitting on a chair, then rest your hands in your lap, palms facing upwards, one hand on top of the other. If you are sitting cross-legged on a cushion or meditation stool this may be uncomfortable so rest the backs of your hands on top of the thighs. The hands don't need to be in some mystical position they just need to be resting comfortably.

Now you are sitting in a comfortable position, the body needs to relax just a little before the start of the meditation session, so empty the lungs by exhaling through the mouth ensuring that there is no more air left in them. Now breathe in through the nose until the lungs are full again and then exhale through the mouth, gently expelling all of the air out of the body again. This exercise needs to be done three times before you start to meditate and the out breath needs to be slower and longer than the in breath. You will then feel your body gently relaxing and you will be ready to start the meditation session. After the three breathing techniques are finished just sit still for a short while, try not to think of any problems or pressing issues in your life. Then when you are ready, start this meditation technique.

Breathe in through the nose using all of your lungs not just the top half, and then breathe out through the nose. This is the normal way a person should be breathing, not just for the purpose of meditation. Just practise this way of breathing for a while if you don't already breathe like this, then, when you are comfortable breathing like this just let the body take over. It will do this automatically and you will no longer have to worry about how you are breathing.

Now, without controlling or interfering with your breathing at all, I want you to be aware that you are breathing in through the nose and out through the nose. You should just be watching your breath as if you are standing to one side and casually observing what is going on. If you find this difficult and are unable to maintain this focus, be aware that there are places the breath passes as you breathe in that you could focus on to make the meditation easier. There is a point at the back of the nose that you will be able to feel as the air passes it. Focus on this point when you breathe in. When filling the lungs with air, the belly will start to expand outwards. You can also use this as a focal point of the meditation or use them both if it helps. On the 'out' breath the belly will contract and start to move inwards, use this as a focal point when breathing out. The air that you are breathing out will pass the end of the nostrils. You should be able to feel this, so use this as another focal point for the 'out' breath. Once again, do not interfere with or alter your breathing, you are only watching it.

When meditating for the first couple of weeks, fifteen minute sessions should be long enough. When you get used to meditating you will know when you are ready to stop without looking at the clock. If you feel comfortable meditating for longer periods after this point then just go for it. Meditate twice a day, once in the morning before eating and once in the evening before eating. If you have to eat first, then leave at least two hours before doing any meditation. Once again, meditation only works when you practice it. It will change your life and the way you think. Meditation will give you inner peace and a new perception of how life is around you and where you are going in this life.

Practising meditation will help you to keep a correct perspective on life. It will give stability to the mind which will enable clear and positive thinking. When your thoughts are clear, you will have the ability to take the right course of action when faced with difficult and stressful circumstances. This will apply throughout your life, so when practising meditation, no matter what situations arise, you will find that you will have stability of mind and total confidence in everything you do.

Suicide

When there is no mental.stability or positive thought patterns in the mind, then negative thought patterns will emerge and involuntary irrational thinking will occur. This may cause stress throughout both the mind and the body. When our body and mind are under stress, it can make decision-making difficult, being indecisive will take away our confidence and cloud our judgement. Sometimes indecision and the loss of confidence will lead to greater stress and we develop feelings of loneliness and despair within ourselves. Even when family, friends and loved ones are around us, the feeling of helplessness and loneliness will still be there inside. When it becomes apparent to others that there is something wrong, they will try to help by giving comfort and what they feel is good advice but this will not ease the pain because the problems we have lie within. Given time most people will eventually overcome their problems, but others just learn to live with them and carry on with life the best they can.

There are however some people who are unable, either through ignorance or the inability to control their emotions, to overcome the feeling of ever-growing stress and unhappiness. The majority of these people, and the numbers are growing, decide that enough is enough; they feel that they cannot put up with their loneliness or depression any longer, and they decide to take their own life. Almost without exception, the problem that these people have within their lives is not the reason that they commit suicide. The reason is incorrect thinking. It is not the problems that these people have that make them want to kill themselves; it is the way they deal with these problems. If they handle their situation badly then their clarity of thought clouds over and they are not able think in a clear and positive way. When this happens, the process of irrational thinking takes over. Although taking one's life is wrong, for them, it would seem quite feasible and the right thing to do. They may wonder why they never thought of it before. It is the perfect solution to all of their problems. Committing suicide would, it seems, be the easiest and most preferable solution.

Unfortunately for the people who do commit suicide, it is not the easy way out. In fact, it is not a way out at all. We are all here for a reason and we can't just opt out of an unhappy situation when we feel like it.

We are all allocated a certain amount of time to achieve the things that we set ourselves to do before we came to this planet. If we shorten that time, then that time will have to be made up and any lessons left unlearnt will have to be repeated. What this means is that we will have to come to the Earth once again to re-learn the same lessons that we struggled with when we were here previously. Then there will be extra lessons added on because we will need to learn that suicide is wrong. We cannot just drop out of a class when we feel like it. When this is understood, we can then move on with our life.

There are many reasons why some people consider suicide. It is not just stress and unhappiness that drive them to do it. There are also people suffering with severe illness and others with relentless pain who feel that they have just had enough and are no longer prepared to put up with the amount of suffering that they are going through.

It is very easy to see their point of view but one must look at the whole picture. Nobody is ever given more than they can handle when they come down to the Earth to learn. No lesson is too hard or so far out of reach that a person is unable to achieve it. No illness or pain will be so great that a person can no longer bear it. In fact, it may be the very reason why that person has come down here to the Earth. The suffering of illness, pain, stress and unhappiness and the countless other challenges people have to go through, may be the very lessons that they have come here to learn. There would be no point in giving people lessons or goals that were unobtainable, that would be ridiculous. If you are a person who feels that you are at your wits end and may be considering suicide as an option to end the suffering you are going through, then think again. If you decide to go through with it, you will not only be delaying the inevitable, you will also be adding more suffering to your lot.

There have been a lot of incidents over the past few years of people helping others to commit suicide. There are also some countries that are quite happy to allow this kind of practice to take place on their soil. They even condone the setting up of organisations that promote the taking of life and whom will also take a fee for arranging it. This is very wrong, even though it is heart-breaking to stand by and watch a loved one suffer in pain as they die from cancer, or maybe from dementia, or from some other insidious disease. Taking the life of a person before that life is ready to end, is against the universal law of nature. To take the life of the person who is suffering, will not only cut short the lessons that that person is learning but it will also mean that they will have an extra life to re-learn those lessons.

Unfortunately it doesn't stop there because by taking the life of another, whether it is for compassionate reasons or not, brings into play the laws of karma. This is the universal law of cause and effect. The laws of karma are quite simple. They state that if a person causes harm, distress or unauthorised interference to someone else's life, then that person will at some stage have to pay for that wrong doing. If someone helps another by giving love, kindness, or even financial help, without doing the good deed for reward or recognition, then that person will at some stage receive a good deed, in some form or another, back to themselves.

So, we now know that to commit suicide, or have someone else do it for you if you are incapable of doing it yourself, is not only wrong but the cost of doing so is too expensive in both time wasted and in the extra lessons and suffering that will be added on.

So what is the best way of preventing a person having suicidal tendencies? Show them that they can change the way they think. We can do this by teaching them Meditation.

Tough Times Ahead

Fate

There are many people who believe in fate. What they mean is that they believe that everybody's life is mapped out before they are born, so that when we start our journey here, our destiny has already been foretold. The events in our life have already been pre-determined before we enter the physical body, e.g. this is where we are going, this is how we get there and this is what will happen on the journey.

If this was the case, then what would be the purpose of life? There would be no point coming here just to live out our life as if it were a stage show in a theatre, just learning the lines and taking the bow at the end. There is no script that we have to adhere to while we are here. Admittedly there are some things that are automated in our lives otherwise we wouldn't be able to function properly. The functions of most of our bodily organs are regulated for us throughout our lives. If this were not the case, we would have to spend so much time operating them manually that we wouldn't get anything else done. It would have to become our life's work and thereby defeat our learning process here on Earth.

We all come down here for a reason. As I have said before, the Earth is a place where we come to learn. We all have a list of things that we need to learn when we come here but how we learn them is left for us to experience. It is not a foregone conclusion that we will succeed with everything on the list. If we are unable to complete or fail in our attempts to learn some of the items on the present list, then those items will be added to a new list of things we will need to learn when we are ready to come back here again. Many of things that we need to learn while we are here will be extremely difficult so, if that degree of difficulty is taken away by fate, then the results will mean nothing.

I must emphasise that every lesson that has been set for us to learn while we are here, will be learnt by our own efforts and experience. The results that we are working towards will be achieved by our own merits. Whether fate is believed or not, has nothing whatsoever to do with us living our life here on the Earth.

While we are here, the way we live this life and the actions we take to learn our lessons are governed by the universal laws of cause and effect ('karma'). If we tread over others to achieve our own goals, then be prepared for some unpleasant payback. If on the other hand we help others to achieve their goals and we are generally considerate towards others, then be prepared for a better form of payback. The universal laws of cause and effect will affect us throughout our lives, and has absolutely nothing to do with fate.

Pride

One of the things that I have noticed over the past few years, and even more so in recent times, is that it seems to be difficult for some people to admit to being wrong. This is not just a male or just a female problem as both are guilty of this trait.

There are a number of reasons why this happens and pride is probably the most common reason. Nobody likes to be proven wrong and it can hurt one's pride if being wrong is not handled properly. Pride is one of the tools that we are given to use while we are here. Pride can play a big part in our lives but when it is over-used, it can beset us with all sorts of other problems that we will need to overcome if we are to progress further.

When used properly pride is a useful tool. None more so than when we have reached a milestone or achieved a goal in our life and are able to take pride in the way we handled this achievement. If we have created something of beauty we can feel a great deal of pride in the hard work that went into the creation of our masterpiece. Pride helps us to realise the greatness of our own life achievements but we can also take pride in the achievements of others. The pride that we have in our children when they achieve high grades in their 'A' level exams or if they are accepted for a place at university and also when finally they receive their degree and graduate from university and take the first step on the ladder of their chosen career. We can also take pride in ourselves when our children grow up to be not only our siblings but our friends as well.

If pride is not handled correctly then it could be the reason why we have to keep coming back to this world. It could be the very thing that is stopping us from moving forward and progressing on to the next stage of our lives. The emotion we call pride can turn a quiet evenly-balanced person into somebody who is full of rage and has so much anger within them that they completely lose control of all normal reasoning. This anger, if it is not stopped, can easily turn into physical violence.

Let us look at a situation that we could easily find ourselves in by having a surplus amount of pride and using it to excess.

Jim and Andy are colleagues who both work for an IT company in London that produces hardware products for the computer industry.

Andy is the development department manager and has a team of thirty staff. His team are working on a new project that involves the development of a new design of hard drive which is right at the cutting edge of technology. Andy prides himself on having a great deal of knowledge and experience in this field and likes to work very closely with his staff, overseeing every aspect of the development. The project has run into some difficulties because some of the newly designed components within the hard drive do not appear to be working correctly. This has put quite a strain on Andy and his team as they have a very tight deadline to meet and the time allotted for the completion is rapidly ticking away.

On the other hand, Jim has different skills. He is the sales manager for the company and has a team of twenty staff.

Although Andy is very experienced at his job, he knows very little about what goes on in other parts of the company, whereas Jim has to have some knowledge of all aspect of the company's business. This means that Jim's knowledge of the company's products, including any new developments and the manufacturing process of these products, are always up to date. He would also have knowledge about the pricing structure of the company's products so that if their competitors lowered their prices, he would be responsible for any discounts that are offered to his company's customers, while making sure that the company would still make a profit from the discounted transactions.

Having knowledge in every aspect of the company's business means that Jim is a great asset to the company so, from time to time, he is asked by the director of operations to help out in other departments that are experiencing problems.

Jim was sent along to Andy's department to see if he could add any input to help solving the problems that they were experiencing with the hard drive components. Andy had been informed by the director of operations that Jim was on his way to his department. When Jim arrived he got a very cold reception from Andy. Andy felt that he, being the specialist in this field and also one of the designers, was more than capable of handling the situation and he didn't need a salesman coming into his department telling him how to do his job.

There were heated discussions every time Jim suggested a possible solution to the component problem and Andy refused to co-operate with him. He talked down any suggestion that Jim made saying that he didn't have the same experience or understanding as a qualified designer.

Jim took everything that Andy said in his stride as he could tell that Andy was struggling with his pride. He told Andy that he had been sent to lend him a hand and was not there to take over his job. He suggested that they look at his proposals calmly and if they were unable to find a solution to the problem then they should put their heads together and pool their knowledge to get the right result. He said pride shouldn't stand in the way of their finding an answer.

Pride is an emotion the can destroy rational thinking. It can take over your life in such a way that all your powers of reasoning just go straight out of the window. When you are faced with a situation where you know that you are wrong and you can admit to that fact, then the amount of relief and satisfaction you can get from that admission is far greater than the amount of stress you will have to go through trying to prove that you are always right.

Don't let pride get in your way. Feel proud when the occasion merits it. Take pride in the things you do and the achievements you earn but remember, pride is just one of the tools we are given while on this world, use it to help achieve the goals you came down here for, not to hinder. It's up to us how we use or abuse this tool.

The Weather and other irritations

Have you ever wondered about our life on Earth? We accept many of the things that happen to us while we are here as being normal, and indeed they are normal for this life, but have you ever thought how strange some of these things are? If we give this subject some thought, it can help us get a better understanding of why we are living here and also why we have to put up with the conditions we are given.

Have you ever thought about the weather systems on our world? We always seem to be complaining about the weather. It is always too hot, too cold, too dry, too wet or too windy. It is always too much or too little of what we would like it to be but then, perhaps, this is because we all have different preferences. The weather never seems to be just right for us and, if on occasion it *is* just right, it only lasts for a day or two.

How about rain! Have you ever really thought about the rain? It just falls right out of the sky, straight down on top of our heads, how primitive is that? Take the following scenario.

You've just spent hours getting ready to attend the most important interview of your working career. To make sure you are not late, you leave your home 30 minutes earlier than you need to. Unfortunately when you arrive at the nearest car park to the company where the interview is taking place, you find that all of the parking spaces are taken. However, all is not lost because you have allowed enough time for a short walk if necessary. You manage to find a place to park which is just a ten minute walk from where the interview is being held. Then, just as you step out of your car, the heavens open. The rain is coming down so heavy that it hurts as it bounces off your head. In desperation you reach inside the car for your umbrella but realise in dismay that you have left it at home. There is not enough time left to sit in the car until the storm passes so you decide to make a run for it but get thoroughly soaked in the process.

You finally reach your destination and drip your way up to the reception desk only to be greeted by the receptionist with "Oh is it raining then?" She shows you into a waiting room where, after a short while, you are joined by three other candidates who are also to be interviewed for the same job and none of whom seem to be the least bit wet. As the last person sits down he looks over in your direction with a wry smile and asks whether you got caught in the rain. Before you can reply the office door opposite opens and you are the first to be called in.

As you walk into the interview room you are greeted by three people sitting behind a long desk and you are invited to sit on the chair positioned in front of the desk. At this point you are feeling very nervous, which is not helped by the fact that you are also soaking wet. After the initial introduction and questioning, which you thought you handled quite well, smiles appear on the faces of all three interviewers. There is a full length mirror on the wall to your right and as you turn your head discreetly in the direction of the mirror, to your horror you notice steam slowly rising from the top of your head and clothes. The interview continued but you were lost in the embarrassment of it all.

There is nothing better than the weather to humble us and bring us back down to earth. Here are some more examples:

(i)   the flashy driver in the fast car who feels invincible when he leaves everyone behind as he speeds along the wet road and eventually ends up in the roadside ditch;

(ii)   the climbers who ignore the weather warnings and the good advice they are given yet still go ahead and climb the mountain because they think they know better, get caught in a blizzard on the mountain top, and have to rely on others putting their lives at risk to rescue them;

(iii)   the reckless sailors who ignore the red flags and go out sailing when the shipping forecast announces storm-force winds and have to be rescued while clinging onto their expensive up-turned yachts.

This planet and its weather systems have been designed in such a way that it can offer us a wealth of opportunities to learn from. Instead of complaining about the weather we should grasp with open arms the opportunities that it presents to us, as well as being appreciative for the insight and learning that we will gain from the experiences we will encounter. Sometimes we will be playing the victim and sometimes we will be the hero. It can bring a rich person to poverty in the twinkling of an eye or equally give those who are poorer, notoriety and riches.

Something I have noticed over the years is that everything we do, feel and experience, in fact, every occasion and meaningful thought that we have ever had, is a part of the lesson we are here to learn.

Let us look at something ordinary that happens to almost everybody during their lifetime.

Long-sightedness

This happens to many people throughout the world. As soon as we reach middle age our eyesight starts to change. We are no longer able to read small print so easily and as time goes on it becomes increasingly more difficult to read small print at all, even larger print becomes blurry or fuzzy. Why is this?

I know that there are some people who are born with eyesight problems, there are also people who are born blind but thankfully this type of problem is not very common.

When humans first walked on the Earth, their life expectancy was very low, maybe about thirty five to forty years, so failing eyesight should not have been too much of a problem. If it did occur, then it would have only been a short-term inconvenience. In modern times as our life expectancy has increased, it wouldn't be too unfair to expect that the efficiency of our eyes would also last longer. Do you realise that if the average person were to reach the age of eighty years, it would mean that for half of their lifetime they would have to struggle along with failing eyesight.

Surely our designers should have realised that our life expectancy was bound to increase when they placed a brain inside our head that has the capacity to expand its intelligence and become technologically more advanced from one generation to the next. It should not have been too difficult to work out that, as an evolving species, we would have become capable of expanding our intellect to such a point that we would be able to improve not only our food production and cleanliness but also our medical expertise, health and living conditions which are all advancements that promote longevity. So why does our eyesight start to fail halfway through our life?

Things are not always as they seem to be. Some of the things that happen to us during our stay on Earth may at first appear to be quite unfair but everything here happens for a reason. I'm sure that our designers were quite capable of providing us with eyes that would be able to last far longer than the lifetime of any human being. They gave us the eyes we have now, not because of any form of malice towards us, but because the eyes we have now offer us the perfect opportunity to be used, not only as a tool for seeing with, but also as a means of learning from. How on earth can we learn anything from our eyes? Well apart from the obvious, there are many things our eyes can teach us when our sight begins to fail.

Patience

Patience is one of the virtues that we can learn from our eyes. It is easy to become impatient with ourselves when we are unable to read the print on the back of packaging when we are shopping, also trying to read the newspaper becomes a challenge when the print appears so blurry that we have to guess the words we are trying to read.

At this point there is a sudden realisation that things are starting to change for us, so the first appointment to the optician is made. This is followed by a severe shock as we learn how much an eyesight test and a pair of glasses will cost us. Our failing eyesight is starting to teach us many things. First and foremost on this occasion, we are learning the true value of our eyesight and what it means when we start to lose it.

We should also take a moment to reflect on other parts of the body that are likely to wear out as we continue to get older. We may begin to feel the effect of failing hearing, aching and worn out joints and also misused diseased organs which will start to cause us pain, discomfort and inconvenience. It is possible that this will also bring home to us the value of learning patience because we will need all the patience we can get as we spend many an hour trying to read the magazines in the waiting room of the doctor's surgery and the out-patient's department of our local hospital.

The above can be avoided in most cases by taking regular exercise, eating healthily and adopting a correct mental attitude. If we can embrace these three values and incorporate them into our life, the lessons that we are learning here will not change but physically we will feel lighter, stronger, more vibrant, less stodgy and more pro-active. Mentally we will be able to think more clearly and concentrate easier and for longer periods. These attributes will give us a better chance to overcome many of the challenges that our life lessons will present us with. Our attitude to life will also change. It will make us stronger and give us a more positive outlook on life.

Using these principles will also be beneficial for us throughout our life as we are more likely to be healthier, fitter and less prone to the illness patterns and stress that we hold within our body.

Relaxation and correct breathing is also vitally important and which I shall talk about later in this book.

As we get older and if we continue to use the three principles of regular exercise, healthy eating and adopting a correct mental attitude (as mentioned above), we should be able to maintain our health both physically and mentally, then when it is time for us to leave this world we will do so without too much suffering. It is better to die feeling fit and healthy rather than live out the last few years of our life with ill-health, disability or pain. So, the next time you sit down to eat the third burger and chips of the week, or finish off the third pint of the evening—and it's not even eight o'clock yet—or light up the fifth cigarette of the day before lunchtime, think! You just might be setting yourself up for some *tough times ahead*. Yes, it is true. We *do* create our own reality.

Eating

There is something else I have noticed about our life on Earth that could be thought of as a little strange. For instance, the method we have been given to take sustenance into the body is less than dignified. Surely there must be other ways of introducing the nourishment we need to keep us alive other than devouring portions of plant life and bits of animal. *Have you ever seriously given it any thought*? Eating is obviously something we all have to do if we want to remain living on this world. We have also been given taste buds to make the experience a little more enjoyable and also as a safeguard against eating things that will do us harm. When we listen to the numerous celebrity chefs whose programmes fill our television screens day after day, they would have us believe that eating is an art form and preparing, cooking and presenting us with a plateful of their food, which is not only an artistic creation but also a gastronomic delight, will be the best eating experience we will ever have. It is *what* we eat and *how much* we eat, that keeps our body fit, healthy and functioning properly, not how good it looks on the plate. Actually, eating is a necessity and is the only way that we have been given to refuel our physical body. However, not only do we need vitamins and minerals to sustain our body but we also need 'Chi' if we are to live on this world.

What we need to understand is that it is the type, quality and quantity of food that we put into our body to refuel it that will help to keep it in good working order. Although I am sure there must be better ways of putting nutrition into our body, shovelling food into what is effectively just a hole in our face is the way that we have been given while here on this world. *Is this weird* or is it just me? What do *you* think? Putting food into our body this way may be bizarre but it does offer us another useful tool that we can use to learn from. So, how can we learn from eating?

In today's world we tend to eat on the go, we are living in a fast food, ready meal society. Put it in the microwave, then sling it down our throats, then off we go again on to the next distraction. We tend to lose some of the value that food should give us when we eat these kinds of meals. It may say on the pack "added vitamins and minerals" but the real value of the food is gone. It is pre-prepared, processed dead food, that is to say it doesn't contain any of the life-force energy (Chi) that we find in fresh food and which the body needs to keep itself healthy and which will also help to stem off illness and disease. When we eat this type of food and then rush off to do other things, it puts our body under tremendous stress because we are not stopping to digest after eating. So one of the first lessons we will learn from eating is the pain and discomfort of indigestion, followed up by tiredness and lethargy from eating foods that have no life-force energy left in them.

If we consistently eat too much food and also too much of the wrong kind of foods, we will not be doing ourselves any favours, the truth is we can start expecting health problems to creep up on us at some time in the not too distant future.

Looking from a more positive viewpoint, we will be giving ourselves an opportunity to learn some important extra lessons. We will have the opportunity of experiencing what it is like to be over-weight or even obese, and also how to overcome the problems that being over-weight or obese bring with it. These particular lessons may not be on the list of lessons that we have come to learn on this visit to the Earth, but if these extra lessons interfere with or prevent us from completing our original tasks at this visit because we have been eating incorrectly, then we can expect a few added visits to the Earth to make this time up.

From the above extra lessons we can expect to experience discomfort from carrying larger bulk around on bones that are designed to carry a lighter weight. If we reach the stage of clinical obesity, we will also run the risk of suffering from a number of serious illnesses including diabetes, heart disease and arthritis which could also shorten our life expectancy.

As we have to fuel our body at regular intervals by eating foods which are either, grown, reared or manufactured, and because this food is not meant solely for the purpose of human consumption, there are parts of it that our body cannot use and which will have to be removed lest we shall explode. The way we have been given to remove the waste products that are left when the body has taken what it needs from the food, is an automatic process that is by excreting it out through various orifices either by urination or defecation. You may be forgiven for thinking that this process is not only a little primitive but can also be a little messy. The process of removing waste from our body was not designed for our convenience but as a way of learning important lessons that are private to each of us. Let us look at some examples of these lessons.

Constipation

This is a condition that is not discussed amongst people generally but can have serious consequences if we allow the condition to persist. Embarrassment is a common reason for putting up with this condition. We can feel too embarrassed to go and talk to the doctor about this problem, or too awkward to ask for a remedy at the chemist. This is becoming a common condition in society today, firstly because of the type of foods we eat and secondly because we don't drink enough water. Learn the lesson and overcome any embarrassment that you may be feeling by seeking out any advice necessary. This is only a minor physical condition that can easily be corrected, don't let it get out of hand. Almost everybody will experience constipation at least once in their life.

Flatulence

This is the medical term for passing gas from the digestive system and out through the anus. This gas is mostly made up from hydrogen, methane and carbon dioxide and is usually odourless. A person who suffers from excessive flatulence has, from the beginning of time, been the butt of many a joke. (*No pun intended*). This is a condition that affects everybody on a daily basis and is a normal biological process.

Excessive flatulence can be remedied by a change of diet and lifestyle. Not gulping down our food or drink will also help. Every time we swallow food, drink or saliva we also take down a small amount of air which is made up from mostly oxygen and nitrogen. If we swallow our food or drink too quickly then we take down more air than normal and this causes us to pass wind more often. The process of flatulence is normal but we all hope that it doesn't happen to us when we are in the presence of others, especially when the gases come out too fast and cause embarrassment!

When our bodies were designed, surely there must have been an alternative and more dignified method of expelling these gases, or is it just another reminder of our position in the great scheme of things.

There are many faults that can be identified within the physical and mental body. They may at first be thought of as weaknesses or defects but if we care to take a look beyond the mirror at what we are actually seeing, things may appear very different indeed. When I see the human body I do not see weakness or defects but opportunity. When our body, either mental or physical fails, this means that either one of two things could be happening to it.

- Firstly it fails because we are experiencing a life lesson. This means that the problem we have encountered is happening because it is intended to happen. It is one of the lessons that we have chosen to come to the Earth to learn.

- Secondly, the body can fail because we have abused it in some way either by incorrect diet, smoking, drinking alcohol excessively or taking un-prescribed drugs. Also working excessive hours is another way we can abuse our body as we do need to take a rest from time to time. When we do not exercise our body on a regular basis it will start to complain. We will become weak through lack of exercise and should also expect an increase in our weight. When this happens we should expect to become fatigued more often and sometimes feel too tired to carry out our normal everyday tasks effectively.

It is possible that lethargy may creep in at this point and when this happens it may become too much effort for us to take on any form of the physical responsibility. The next stage is even more serious because we become so lethargic that we really couldn't care less about anything, either what is going on around us or even to us. This, in extreme cases, can quite often leads to a situation where things are so difficult for us that we may even consider suicide.

While we are on this world, our body is the only thing that we can count on to get ourselves around and be able to do the things that we have to do. If we abuse it to the extent that it becomes unable to function properly, it will affect our chances of completing the lessons that we have come here to learn. If this happens then we will have to come back here again and again. For most of us the Earth is not a very pleasant place to live, it is not meant to be, but if we look after ourselves properly we can complete our tasks quickly and then be able to leave this place for good.

We create our own reality

What do I mean by "we create our own reality"? Well it is absolutely true we do create our own reality. When we arrive on Earth we have a list of things to do and within reason it is more or less left up to us how we want to play it. I can already hear you saying "What list?" Well it is the list that makes up our entire life of things to do while we are here on the Earth at this visit. It is a list of all the lessons that we will need to learn and experience during our stay here. I realise that very few people are actually aware of this list and this is because it has been saved into the great library of our subconscious. It is from the subconscious that the items on this list will be made apparent to us as and when the time is right and when it is deemed we are ready to start learning.

As I have already mentioned earlier in this book, we are given every chance possible to achieve the lessons we will be expected to learn and experience. We are brought into this world by the parents whom we feel are most likely to bring us up in the way that will give us the right start. We are provided with all the required tools to help us get the job done, one of which includes our body, as outlined above. When our chosen parents have completed the task of our up-bringing, it is then up to us to create our own reality.

So, what do a lot of us do? Light up a cigarette and then nip down to the pub for a few pints and watch the football on the big screen with our mates or spend all day watching TV and playing computer games while grazing on fast foods, cigarettes and drink. It becomes an uphill struggle from then on because this is the reality we have created. It is a reality that a lot of us will live for the rest of our shortened lives and it is this reality that will determine how we will be able to cope with the lessons that are ahead of us. We have a choice, and if we pick the above reality as our choice then we can expect to struggle a little in later life with breathing difficulties, perhaps lung problems like frequent bouts of bronchitis, emphysema and maybe lung cancer. There will be weight problems due to over-eating and excessive drinking of alcohol possibly leading to cirrhosis of the liver. There could also be heart disease due to clogged arteries and high blood pressure.

These are just a few of the possible problems that we could encounter while we are struggling to learn the things that we came here for. Also as already stated, if we live a life that will artificially shorten our allotted lifespan, then our early death will be deemed to be self-inflicted suicide.

So how do we create a new reality for ourselves? A good starting point would be to know what sort of reality we want to live in. What do you want to have, or be, in your life? It is also important to realise that, although it would be nice to be wealthy and have all the trappings that come along with wealth, money isn't everything. In fact it has very little to do with the lessons that most of us have come here to learn, unless we are here specifically to learn how to be wealthy and how to handle money.

Money is the currency that we use to trade with, it is the liquidity of money throughout the world's business that keep the countries of the world flowing. It is also important to understand that everything we possess whether it be financial wealth, property, cars, computers, furniture, absolutely everything, even a toothpick, is just on loan to us for the duration of our stay on Earth. We own nothing and when we leave here the only things we are able take with us are the knowledge and wisdom that have been learned and experienced during our stay. So, we have to be careful what we wish for or we could be leaving here spiritually bankrupt and no wiser than when we arrived. Also, if any of the items on our reality list are in conflict with the lessons that we need to learn, or with the reason for which we came here, then we may not be able to create them into our lives, or if we do, they may make the rest our stay on Earth a difficult one.

Here are some examples that will give us an idea of what we might want to consider creating into our new reality. They are not in any order of importance but for my own personal preference I would choose peace of mind or inner peace as the first thing on my list. It doesn't matter what else is going on in our life, if we don't have peace of mind then every situation that comes our way whether good or bad may affect us on a level that could easily cause us unnecessary stress that could make them more difficult to overcome. Peace of mind will give us the ability to handle any event easily without getting too stressed and without anxiety, thereby bringing any difficult situation to its conclusion much easier and avoiding the need for panic measures being taken.

You may decide to create your new reality by moving to a different area, somewhere that you've always wanted to live. This will mean buying a new house. What would your ideal property be? Maybe you would like a large apartment or perhaps a house or bungalow. Whatever property you want, visualise yourself already living there, see yourself standing outside in front of it, look at every detail. What type of windows does it have? What colour are they and how many? Is the front door wooden with glass in it, or is it painted without glass? Does the property have a front garden, if so, is it a big garden well planted with flowers and shrubs or perhaps it may be covered with block paving? Pay close attention to all the details and remember them because what you visualise is what you will get.

Carry out the same process with the back of the property and then move inside and look at every room in the same detail. See it as you want it to be, visualise the design of every room, the furniture, the decoration, whether it has an inglenook fireplace etc. Make a drawing of the property with a plan view of each room and include where you would put the furniture. Make notes of how the decoration will look, see your new home in every detail and believe it is yours, you are already living there.

Now all you have to do is take some action you must turn this visualisation into an actualisation. The universe will give you what you want but you must put in some work as well. For instance, you cannot get that job of a lifetime if you don't take any action. You must send in your CV first before things start to happen. If there is a gift of a million pounds waiting for you in the room next door, then unless you take action it will stay there. You must open the door and walk through into the room to collect your gift. There may be pitfalls along the way but you must persevere and continue with your commitment to creating your own reality and it will happen—it may not be next week or next month but it will happen in due course.

There are many ways to get the things we want and there is no limit to what is on offer. We can have literally anything we can think of. This opportunity is as big as our imagination but there are certain rules applied that we have to abide by. When we are asking for whatever it is we want, we must always ask for it in the present tense. The universe doesn't understand the past, the past has gone and the universe is unable to work in this time period as it only exists in our memory. It does not recognise the future either as the future has not arrived yet, so, because the future also doesn't exist, the universe is unable to manifest your request from this time period either. The universe only recognises the present and time as we know it to be doesn't really exist.

Our time is governed by the sun and the other planets that orbit around it. It is the gravity produced by the sun and the other planets that regulate the distance we are from the sun and also the speed at which we are travelling around it. It is this gravity that holds us in the orbital position we are in and it is this position that gives us the regular pattern that we recognise as time.

If something happened to the earth that causes it to move the position of its orbit around the sun, then the regular patterns that we are used to would change, and so would our concept of time. The time we are familiar with, is used to give us a sense of order in our lives; it takes away the feeling of drifting around aimlessly through space. We need time to keep order in our lives but the universe doesn't. It is only ever in the present, no matter where it is or where we exist in it, there is no past and no future. The present is the place where we all exist; it is in the present that everything exists and it is in this place that the universe will arrange for us to get what we want.

If we want to manifest emotional things like love, kindness, or inner peace then we would still ask for them in the present tense. If we would like to have some different abilities, then the source of these abilities will only be found in the present. Perhaps we would like good health, then we would ask for it here in the present because that's where we are, the people of this world are all here in the present. What would be the use of giving us health in the future? The future hasn't arrived yet and we might have a critical illness now, here in the present.

We could ask the universe for anything and it will oblige but, whatever it is we ask for, will be provided to us by people. We could say that the universe is the middle man, so when we ask it for something it will say I haven't got that but I know someone who has and it will make the necessary arrangements for it to be delivered. Some of the easier things we want can be manifested quite quickly. An example of this would be to manifest something that we could have just by changing what we do ourselves. Let us say, for instance, you wanted to obtain peace of mind, our friend, the universe, will then point us in the direction of the nearest newsagent where in the local paper you will magically find an advert for, say, meditation classes in your area. Most manifestations of this nature can be delivered quickly because they involve less people and they are physically easy to produce.

Now let us say that we wanted something that is physically more substantial both in size and financial value. I'm thinking maybe a new car, perhaps the car of our dreams, or maybe a bigger house with a few acres of land. To manifest something of this nature is slightly more difficult and will take a little longer to produce. Why should this be? The universe is a powerful machine. It can produce trillions of stars and planets and form them into huge galaxies, a puny little car or house should be no trouble at all? That is exactly right but no matter how powerful the universe is, it can only work with the tools it is given and the tools that it has to work with on Earth are human beings. The world that we are living on is by-and-large a mechanical place, even our newest state of the art technology is electronically mechanical. So, if the universe were to manifest all of our wishes out of thin air, then that would be magic and this is not a world of that nature. Can you imagine how clogged up our roads would be if everybody could manifest the car of their dreams instantly? A country estate with the obligatory mansion on it would be so common-place, there wouldn't be enough room on the planet to fit them all in. So as powerful as the universe is, it can only manifest our wants within the parameters laid down by the world they are for. In this case, the parameters are set by the cost, manpower to manufacture the items and people to provide them for us.

So far we have only talked about manifesting the things that we need or think we need, most of the things that are wanted are the material possessions of this world but we can also use manifestation to obtain something else; a different way of life. Yes, we can use manifestation to create our own reality. If we don't like the way that our life is going then we can change it and create another life. It is easily done but don't take it too lightly. It will need a great deal of thought before we do it because we may end up with a life that is not as good as the one we've just left.

Ok, so how do we manifest the things that we would like to have? There are many techniques we could use to get what we want, I don't know if one way is any better than another. I think that it probably comes down to individual preference as to which way works best. A good way to start though is to use affirmations. The way to get started is by having pen and paper to hand and an idea of what it is that you want.

What is it you would like to have? It must be something that you want with a passion. It is no good saying "Well, I would quite like a new bike, car, house, girlfriend/boyfriend or new life—I don't suppose it will ever happen but if it does that will be great". Well, I can tell you now that it won't happen. What is it that you *really* want? You must make a decision as to what it is going to be. Once you have decided and are certain what it is, you can then start the process of getting it.

When using affirmations there are certain rules that you need to abide by. Firstly, everything that you write on your piece of paper will have to be written in the present tense. Secondly, the words that you use must be positive words. If any negative words are used in the affirmation it will bring doubt into your manifestation and, when you keep affirming this negativity, the universe will not understand what you are trying to ask it so it will not work. If for instance you were to write, "I hope that the universe will bring me a bike?" Well it won't. Hope is not a positive word. Also the request you made wasn't written in the present tense. Hope is an in-between word; "I hope that it will happen but I don't know if it will." It should read: "The universe is giving me a bike now." There is nothing in that sentence that is negative and by putting now on the end of it will bring it into the present. This doesn't mean that you will get the bike instantly. Remember, this is not the world of magic. It is a mechanical world and your manifestation will come to you via people, *after* you have taken some action yourself.

When you are writing an affirmation, it will need to be written down at least six times so that it will sink firmly into your subconscious mind because the link between you and the universe is the subconscious mind. Trying to tap into the subconscious is quite difficult because it will not take any notice of what you are saying if you only ask it once. The capacity of the subconscious mind is about nine tenths of the brain. You can liken it to a vast depository of everything that you have ever done, not only in this life, but in past lives also. It keeps a record of everything important connected with the lessons of every lifetime you have ever lived.

The subconscious is also in direct contact with the Higher Self at all times and also relays all important messages that it receives from the Higher Self to the conscious part of the brain so that you can receive direction and guidance that will keep you on the right path. Unfortunately most of us do not have direct access to the subconscious or the information stored in it. So, when writing down the things that you want, you must be persistent and keep affirming the request so that it sinks deep into the subconscious mind where it will then begin to understand what it is that you require it to tell you. It will then get the ball rolling and liaise with the universe to manifesting what you want.

When we have manifested and received whatever it is we want, it doesn't end there. We must also take on the responsibility for the manifestations that we have created.

If say, for instance, we have created our new reality but sense that in this new life there is something that just doesn't feel quite right, it is our creation and we now have to take on the responsibility for it. Maybe our new reality has taken us out of our comfort zone and given us more commitments than we realised it would. Or, maybe we have just asked for too much and, now that we have what we asked for, we are unable to handle it and it wasn't really what we wanted in the first place. We just got greedy. Well it is no good moaning about it; it is our responsibility and no one else's. It is now up to us to stop complaining and just get on and live it.

Does this sound familiar? While out walking you meet an old friend and politely enquire as to how he or she is getting on. "Oh not so bad, things could be worse" they reply with a sigh and then promptly go on for hours telling you how everything is wrong in their life. Well, as we all create our own reality, we are also responsible for the reality that we create, which of course also includes the life that we are living right now. We should understand that if we are not happy with our lot, we should stop moaning and start creating another reality that we will be happier with.

There are many other ways to manifest the things that we want, be it a single item or a whole new life. The Taoist monks (pronounced Daoist) of China use the micro cosmic orbit as a means of manifesting. The micro cosmic orbit has a number of other uses and benefits but when it is being used for manifesting and giving us the things we want, it is a powerful tool indeed and one that I recommend you try.

The method of manifesting that I use quite a lot and with great effect, involves the use of life-force energy (Chi). There is a triangle shaped object called the Unan pattern which can be found in many places around the world. It is not clear where this pattern originated but it is a very ancient pattern that can be seen drawn on walls and in temples in many countries. This pattern is placed by visualisation in the middle of a cupped hand and whatever it is that you want to manifest is then placed inside the middle of the Unan pattern, again by visualisation. Then life-force energy is run through the hands and into the Unan pattern while repeating an affirmation of what it is you want at least six times, using positive words and making sure that what you are saying is in the present tense.

When saying what it is you want, you will need to say it with as much vigour and enthusiasm as possible so that your request will start winging its way to the universe where it will be manifested as soon as humanly possible. Remember, repeating your request at least six times seems to be the number of times it takes for the subconscious mind to take notice of what you are saying.

How you phrase and affirm what it is that you want is quite important. I will not go into more detail about how to manifest as this is not a book solely about manifestation but I will give you a few ideas of words that will help you put together an affirmation.

As I mentioned above, when affirming what it is that you want, it must be said with some real enthusiasm and come straight from your heart. Write it down then say it at least six times with feeling. Your thinking must be light and positive, smile inwardly, smile outwardly and be happy with what you are doing. You are manifesting something that you have always wanted and you know now that you will get it. This is a great moment in your life. You could be making a whole new way of life for yourself. Now, isn't that an exciting thought? I know that when I created a new reality for myself, I thought how fantastic it was that everybody is capable of doing this. If only everybody would put aside their negative thoughts and cynicism, their world could change beyond all recognition and for the better, and they would still be learning the things that they came here for but in a more pleasant and positive way.

'*I*' and '*now*' are good positive words to start a manifestation as they put your request in the present. The word '*now*' can also be used in the middle or at the end of your affirmation. Here are some simple examples:

- '*I create the new reality I want now,*'
- '*I now have complete peace of mind.*'

- *'I have the power now to manifest everything I want.'*

'*I am*' is also a positive affirmation, so affirm:

- *'I am now a very popular person and everyone enjoys my company.'*
- *'I am earning more money now than I ever dreamed possible.'*

I hope that your dreams are big because you will get exactly what you ask for. These are just a few of the examples that can be used when manifesting. So, don't forget, write it down so that you can check exactly what and how you are affirming. Is it in the present and written in a positive way that will make sense to the universe? Say it as if you really mean it. There is no limit to the amount things that you can manifest, just go for it and enjoy the experience.

As It Is

There are many of us who are not aware that life on Earth is a journey. I know that we are travelling around our Sun at about 66,000 miles an hour and our Sun is also travelling around the centre of our galaxy at an even more unbelievable speed, but the travelling I am referring to is the path that we all traverse during our stay on Earth. When we are navigating along the path of life, it is easy to feel that sometimes we are falling by the wayside, or that's how it seems, but on our journey through life we are never left on our own, even though sometimes we may think we are.

When we are beset with the problems that our life on Earth presents us with, there is always someone looking out for us even when we are at our lowest ebb. We can at times feel that there is no way out of the predicament we find ourselves in but there is always help at hand. No one is ever given more to bear than they can handle. There will always be someone there to guide us and pick us up when we fall and feel that we cannot go on any further.

Have you noticed that when the conditions in our life become almost unbearable, within a very short time of reaching this low point, things start to change? There is a reversal of our situation and we can see small changes occurring, it may be something that we have done after receiving help from an inspirational thought or maybe we have acted on advice given by a family member, friends or even a stranger. Gradually there is a turn-around in our fortunes and things start to get better for us. When these changes occur, our mood and outlook on life begins to alter, this is due to the increase of the body's vibrational frequency. When this frequency rises within us then our life seems to be worth living again.

Inspirational thoughts

On occasion we may have a problem that needs to be sorted out or perhaps we want to know the answer to an important question we may have asked. We can receive the answer we are waiting for in one of two ways.

The first way is to retrieve it from our memory. We are able to replay previous knowledge and experiences from which the information we are seeking may be stored. The storage area for information not in current use is in our subconscious mind and can be retrieved by bringing it forward to the forefront of our conscious mind where we can access it when needed.

These are the memories of experiences and information that we have collected but do not need in our everyday life and so are stored in the subconscious mind. The subconscious mind is a database that holds everything we have ever experienced or learnt throughout our life. It is nine times bigger than our conscious mind.

- **The conscious mind** is the part of the brain that deals with life on a day-to-day basis and would soon get bogged down if it had to remember and record every single thing we have ever done. The conscious mind is able to calculate, enabling us to make decisions. It gives us the ability to choose what is right from wrong and which course of action to take when faced with choices. It helps us to express our artistic values and gives us the ability to interact with our fellow human beings.

- **The subconscious mind** on the other hand is a vast repository of information that neither cares whether we access it or not. It has no thinking abilities and makes no decisions; it just stores information either from us or our Higher Self. It is like a stubborn librarian that needs to be asked several times before it will give up the information it holds.

The second way is through Inspirational thoughts.

Inspirational thoughts, however, do not come from our memory. These are thoughts that are live and come to us from our guides, helpers or our Higher Self. Inspirational thoughts are given to us so that we are able get through sticky patches that may be occurring in our life right now. When we receive inspirational thoughts they lift the frequency of our body's vibration to a slightly higher level for a while. This is just enough to carry us through any problems we may be having and are preventing us from moving on any further in our life.

Have you noticed that as we go through life, sometimes we are happy and life feels good, everything is easy for us and things come to us when we want them and without any effort on our part? This is great but, unfortunately, situations like this do not last for ever and before very long the bubble bursts and our fortunes turn completely around the other way. We may wake up one morning feeling a little jaded, the spark seems to have gone from our life and things are not as easy as they were previously. We have to put more of an effort into getting the things we want and doing the things we need to do. Life is suddenly fraught with problems that seem insurmountable and all we want is the sunshine back in our life again.

After waking up to the same old problems day in and day out and unable to see a way through them, we may suddenly be given a quiet moment in our mind when we are able to ask the question that we now feel *able* to ask.

"What can I do to get out of this mess?" There is a quiet moment of relief as we sit there expectantly because, just by asking this question, we know that we have taken the first step forward to change the difficult situation that we find ourselves in.

For a short while we continue on with our life, and all its demands, although we will still feel a little lift because of the small release of tension we received when we asked for help. Then one day during a quiet time when we are able to rest for a while, one of those rare occasions re-occur when we are able to quieten our mind just for a second, and all of a sudden there is a sign of recognition in our mind. It is very quiet, almost undetectable, it may not even be mentally audible and it could just be a feeling. Nevertheless, it is an answer. Sometimes it may not even be the complete answer. Maybe it is just a suggestion or guidance of what we needed to do but make no mistake, it will be the answer to the question that we asked during our hour of need.

As I have mentioned previously in this book, to hear or perceive inspirational thoughts we must develop our sense of intuition. We can develop this intuitive sense by quietening the random thoughts that continually plague our mind. This can be achieved by regularly practising meditation. When our mind becomes quiet, we will be open to receive all the wonders that the universe has to offer. All we have to do is to just wait and listen.

The answer to our question will have come from one of our guides or a helper, or maybe even our Higher Self. This answer would have been sent to us perhaps to give us the vital information or instruction that we would need to help us to climb out of the hole we find ourselves in. It will point us in the right direction and help us overcome the sticking point that may be preventing us from moving further along the path of our life. These are what are called inspirational thoughts. These inspirational thoughts are sent to us from elsewhere. They are not from our own minds nor are they from our previous experiences that have been recorded and stored in our subconscious.

Our Universe

The universe we live in is a vast place, so-much-so that its vastness is beyond our comprehension. The most distant objects from us that we are able to detect are called Quasars. Quasars are so far away that they can only be seen by taking long exposure photographs with large telescopes. Quasars are associated with black holes and colliding galaxies and are known to be the brightest objects in the universe but their size is not much bigger than our solar system. The furthest Quasars can be as far away as 28 billion light years from the Earth and it is thought that these objects were formed in the early history of the universe not long after the occurrence of the Big Bang which, at a guess, should place them fairly close to the edge of our universe, should it not be infinite.

The universe that we live in is a three dimensional universe, it has length, breadth and depth and we, as humans, have been given the equipment to be able to detect these dimensions. Everything in this universe comes from the same source, the Big Bang. The whole of this universe exists because it was made from the elements produced by the Big Bang. There are ninety two naturally occurring elements in our universe and everything is made up from various combinations of these elements. This means that the Sun, Earth and our neighbouring planets are made from the same materials as the suns and planets that are spread across the whole of the universe. The recipe may be in slightly different proportions but the ingredients will be the same.

A singularity outside of our own universe could be programmed with a different set of parameters, so that when a big bang occurs from this singularity it will produce natural elements of a different type to the elements we have here in this universe. This will then give rise to a completely unique and diverse set of conditions and the creation of a new universe. The makeup of the natural elements and their vibrational frequency will produce within this new universe, new and diverse forms of life with different lessons and challenges to experience. The people of this new universe will be given a different set of tools and an added dimension to help them conquer the demands that their new home will place upon them.

These challenges will be totally different to those set for us in this universe. The creation of this new universe may well be the next step forward for many of the developing life forms within our universe to move on to.

It has been written about, and there has been much talk of, a parallel universe that runs alongside our own universe. It is said to be a place where we all have a human double living an opposite life to the one we live here. I can only assume that this means that a person living on Earth in our universe, and whose life may be one of kindness to others i.e. a positive life, will differ from that of our double's life on the Earth in the opposite or parallel universe, in as much that they will be living a life of greed and unkindness to others i.e. a negative life. Of course, the reverse could also be the truth and possibly is.

This may be exciting material for a good science fiction book or an 'out of this world' feature film but if we were able to devote a little more time looking *within ourselves* and asking questions, along with developing our power of intuition, we would soon discover that this is precisely all it is, just far-fetched material that will give us a means of escape from the sometimes mundane routine of our everyday life.

There is a vast area which, although outside of our universe is also very much connected to it. It is in this area which we mistakenly call *Heaven* that we make our temporary home when we are away from the Earth.

Although it is only a temporary home, we actually live there a very long time by Earth standards. Our stay in *Heaven* is slotted in between the many lives that we live on Earth and the countless other planets spread around this universe. We may stay in *Heaven* for many hundreds of years at a time and during this period we will take the opportunity to rest for a while and recuperate from the shock of our previous life on the Earth. Then, soon after we have recovered, we will meet with our guides and spiritual helpers and begin to evaluate the lessons, experiences, the trauma and drudgery of our last life on Earth. After this evaluation we, along with our Higher Self, guides and spiritual helpers, will start to make detailed plans for our next life and where and how we shall live it, be it on Earth or elsewhere in the universe. We will also spend some time receiving people who are returning from the Earth and helping them recover from their ordeal. It would seem that there isn't any respite for us whether we are on Earth or not.

We may make thousands of visits to the Earth and other planets around the universe in our quest to learn and evolve, but we will always return to our spiritual home when our physical lives have ended. We think of our home on the spiritual plane as *Heaven* because we have subconscious memories of being there. It is such a wonderful place that surely it is the home of God. In truth we are much too far down the ladder to have any concept of the real God but, what we experience when we are staying there, is a far greater sense of community, togetherness and spiritual well-being than we could ever experience while we are on the Earth. This is why many of us look forward to returning. Everybody else just thinks that when you're dead, you're dead!

Our spiritual home is divided into hundreds of different areas. Each area is truly vast compared to the size of this universe. All living beings of a compatible nature irrespective of their race will live together in peace, for we are only able to be with those who have a similar vibrational frequency to our own. It is a place of stability and harmony for all who live there. Peace of mind amongst all beings in the spiritual realm is a natural condition.

It is not surprising that we find it difficult to return to this universe to pursue our continuing quest for knowledge. This seems to be our lot at this stage of our existence. The pressures that are exerted on us to return to the Earth must be considerable. Let's face it, who in their right mind would want to leave *Heaven* knowing that a return visit to the Earth can only mean suffering and hardship, lifetime after lifetime.

Our spiritual body is not able to enter the spiritual realm while still occupying the physical body. This is because our physical body's vibrational frequency is not compatible with the frequency there. The spiritual realm has a much higher frequency than that of our physical body so it is impossible for the two to meet. Our spiritual body or soul is able to lower its own frequency just enough to make it compatible to occupy the physical body on Earth but, as soon as the lifespan is over, it will leave it here, and can then raise its own frequency again and so be able to return back to the spiritual realm *Heaven*.

There is much to learn when we visit this universe and in this book I have only just scratched the surface. The more we come to this and other worlds, the closer we will be to the next rung on the ladder and the sooner we will be able to leave this troubled world behind for good.

*   *   *

About the Author

While still in his early twenties the author realised that there was more to life than society was offering and so took it upon himself to find the truth about why we are here on this world. He was guided towards the martial arts from which he learnt self-discipline, self-control and confidence. After studying various religions he was led towards meditation and then contemplation, through which he gained a better understanding of why we need to be on the Earth. He now teaches students this new-found knowledge and, through his Energy Healing Practice, he teaches the importance of life-force energy.